TEACHER'S PET PUBLICATIONS

LITPLAN TEACHER PACK
for
Dracula
based on the book by
Bram Stoker

Written by
Susan R. Woodward

© 2006 Teacher's Pet Publications
All Rights Reserved

This **LitPlan** for
Dracula
has been brought to you by Teacher's Pet Publications, Inc.

Copyright Teacher's Pet Publications 2006

Only the student materials in this unit plan (such as worksheets, study questions, and tests) may be reproduced multiple times for use in the purchaser's classroom.

For any additional copyright questions,
contact Teacher's Pet Publications.

www.tpet.com

TABLE OF CONTENTS - *Dracula*

Introduction	5
Unit Objectives	7
Reading Assignment Sheet	8
Unit Outline	9
Study Questions (Short Answer)	13
Answer Key to Study Questions	21
Quiz/Study Questions (Multiple Choice)	42
Answer Key to Multiple Choice Questions	80
Pre-reading Vocabulary Worksheets	83
Vocabulary Answer Key	109
Lesson One (Introductory Lesson)	113
Oral Reading Evaluation Form	117
Non-Fiction Reading Assignment	118
Group Presentation Evaluation Form	125
Writing Assignment 1: informational	130
Writing Assignment 2: creative/personal	137
Writing Assignment 3: persuasive	154
Peer Editing Form	157
Writing Evaluation Form	155
Vocabulary Review Activities	148
Extra Writing Assignments/Discussion ?s	150
Individual Presentation Evaluation Form	160
Unit Review Activities	161
Unit Tests	167
Unit Resource Materials	203
Vocabulary Resource Materials	223

A FEW NOTES ABOUT THE AUTHOR
Bram Stoker

On November 8, 1847, Abraham (Bram) Stoker was born in a small town near Dublin, Ireland. Bram Stoker suffered from a long childhood illness that kept him weak most of the time, and he was not even able to walk until he was eight years old. After spending his entire early childhood in bed, and after doctors had used leeches in an attempt to cure his illness, it is understandable that the adult Stoker's *Dracula* would contain themes of rising from the dead and blood-letting. It is also understandable that Stoker made up for lost time by becoming an outstanding athlete.

Upon Stoker's miraculous recovery, he went on to lead a healthy life which included participating in sports at Trinity College at the University of Dublin. He graduated in 1868 with a Master's degree in Mathematics, but his heart was not in that field. Stoker's passion was the theatre, and he wanted to be an actor. At his family's urging, Bram Stoker worked at Dublin Castle as a clerk even though it was not what he really wanted to do.

In 1871, Stoker began writing theatre reviews for the Dublin Evening Mail. Although he received no compensation for his work, it was a creative outlet for his passion. Stoker also began writing and publishing short stories in various magazines. His first story, "The Crystal Cup" (1872), was published by The London Society. This was followed by a four-part serial called "The Chain of Destiny" (1875) and his first novel *The Primrose Path* (1875). While continuing to act as a drama critic, Stoker met the famous actor, Henry Irving, and the two became life-long friends. In 1878, Irving hired Bram Stoker as the manager of his London theatre the Lyceum, and Stoker held that position for the next twenty-seven years.

Before moving to London, however, Bram Stoker managed to woo Florence Balcombe away from playwright Oscar Wilde, and the two were married in Dublin. The Stokers only had one child in their thirty-four year marriage, their son Noel.

While working at the Lyceum Theatre, Stoker continued to write. He published *Under the Sunset*, a collection of short stories, in 1881, and he followed with the novels *The Snake's Pass* (1890), *The Watter's Mou'* (1895), and *The Shoulder of Shasta* (1895). It was in 1897 that Stoker published his masterpiece, *Dracula*. Although he continued to write throughout his lifetime, none of his other works received the praise or popularity as his chilling tale of the mysterious Transylvanian Count.

When Stoker's friend and mentor Henry Irving died in 1905, his death supposedly caused Stoker to have a stroke. Although in failing health, Stoker continued to write, and he published, among others, *Personal Reminiscences of Henry Irving* (1906) and *The Lair of the White Worm* (1911). Stoker died on April 20th, 1912.

INTRODUCTION

This LitPlan has been designed to develop students' reading, writing, thinking, and language skills through exercises and activities related to *Dracula*. It includes 24 lessons, supported by extra resource materials.

The **introductory lesson** introduces students to the nineteenth century gothic genre. Following the introductory activity, students are given a transition to explain how the activity relates to the book they are about to read. Following the transition, students are given the materials they will be using during the unit. At the end of the lesson, students begin the pre-reading work for the first reading assignment.

The **reading assignments** are approximately thirty pages each; some are a little shorter while others are a little longer. Students have approximately 15 minutes of pre-reading work to do prior to each reading assignment. This pre-reading work involves reviewing the study questions for the assignment and doing some vocabulary work for 10 vocabulary words they will encounter in their reading.

The **study guide questions** are fact-based questions; students can find the answers to these questions right in the text. These questions come in two formats: short answer or multiple choice. The best use of these materials is probably to use the short answer version of the questions as study guides for students (since answers will be more complete), and to use the multiple choice version for occasional quizzes.

The **vocabulary work** is intended to enrich students' vocabularies as well as to aid in the students' understanding of the book. Prior to each reading assignment, students will complete a two-part worksheet for 10 vocabulary words in the upcoming reading assignment. Part I focuses on students' use of general knowledge and contextual clues by giving the sentence in which the word appears in the text. Students are then to write down what they think the words mean based on the words' usage. Part II nails down the definitions of the words by giving students dictionary definitions of the words and having students match the words to the correct definitions based on the words' contextual usage. Students should then have an understanding of the words when they meet them in the text.

After each reading assignment, students will go back and formulate answers for the study guide questions. Discussion of these questions serves as a **review** of the most important events and ideas presented in the reading assignments.

After students complete reading the work, there is a **vocabulary review** lesson which pulls together all of the fragmented vocabulary lists for the reading assignments and gives students a review of all of the words they have studied.

Following the vocabulary review, a lesson is devoted to the **extra discussion questions/writing assignments**. These questions focus on interpretation, critical analysis and personal response, employing a variety of thinking skills and adding to the students' understanding of the novel.

There is a **group theme project** in this unit. Student groups will select a 19th century Gothic author from a predetermined list. Each group will complete a brief biographical sketch of the author, read two short works (short stories) by the author, and complete a group poster (this last collective effort will be completed in class). The groups will present their information and explain how the literary works by this author fit the gothic genre.

There are three **writing assignments** in this unit, each with the purpose of informing, persuading, or expressing personal opinions. In the first assignment, students will read two stories and discuss the authors' use of the "gothic" elements. In assignment number two, students will create a journal for characters not directly heard from in the novel. In the third writing assignment, students will write a letter explaining their position on teaching Gothic/Horror literature in school.

There is a **nonfiction reading assignment**. Students must read nonfiction articles, books, etc. to gather information about 19th century ideas and concepts.

The **review lesson** pulls together all of the aspects of the unit. The teacher is given four or five choices of activities or games to use which all serve the same basic function of reviewing all of the information presented in the unit.

The **unit test** comes in two formats: multiple choice or short answer. As a convenience, two different tests for each format have been included. There is also an advanced short answer unit test for advanced students.

There are additional **support materials** included with this unit. The **Unit Resource Materials** section includes suggestions for an in-class library, crossword and word search puzzles related to the novel, and extra worksheets. There is a list of **bulletin board ideas** which gives the teacher suggestions for bulletin boards to go along with this unit. In addition, there is a list of **extra class activities** the teacher could choose from to enhance the unit or as a substitution for an exercise the teacher might feel is inappropriate for his/her class. **Answer keys** are located directly after the **reproducible student materials** throughout the unit. The **Vocabulary Resource Materials** section includes similar worksheets and games to reinforce the vocabulary words.

The **level** of this unit can be varied depending upon the criteria on which the individual assignments are graded, the teacher's expectations of his/her students in class discussions, and the formats chosen for the study guides, quizzes and test. If teachers have other ideas/activities they wish to use, they can usually easily be inserted prior to the review lesson.

The student materials may be reproduced for use in the teacher's classroom without infringement of copyrights. No other portion of this unit may be reproduced without the written consent of Teacher's Pet Publications, Inc.

UNIT OBJECTIVES - *Dracula*

1. Through reading Bram Stoker's *Dracula*, students will be gain a better understanding of the 19th century Gothic novel.

2. Students will demonstrate their understanding of the text on four levels: factual, interpretive, critical and personal.

3. Students will study the themes of good vs. evil, fear, love, and compassion.

4. Students will be given the opportunity to practice reading aloud and silently to improve their skills in each area.

5. Students will answer questions to demonstrate their knowledge and understanding of the main events and characters in *Dracula* as they relate to the author's theme development.

6. Students will enrich their vocabularies and improve their understanding of the novel through the vocabulary lessons prepared for use in conjunction with the novel.

7. The writing assignments in this unit are geared to several purposes:
    a. To have students demonstrate their abilities to inform, to persuade, or to express their own personal ideas
    Note: Students will demonstrate ability to write effectively to <u>inform</u> by developing and organizing facts to convey information. Students will demonstrate the ability to write effectively to <u>persuade</u> by selecting and organizing relevant information, establishing an argumentative purpose, and by designing an appropriate strategy for an identified audience. Students will demonstrate the ability to write effectively to <u>express personal ideas</u> by selecting a form and its appropriate elements.
    b. To check the students' reading comprehension
    c. To make students think about the ideas presented by the novel
    d. To encourage logical thinking
    e. To provide an opportunity to practice good grammar and improve students' use of the English language.

8. Students will read aloud, report, and participate in large and small group discussions to improve their public speaking and personal interaction skills.

READING ASSIGNMENT SHEET - *Dracula*

Date Assigned	Chapters Assigned	Date Completed
	1-2	
	3-4	
	5-6	
	7-8	
	9-10	
	11-12	
	13-14	
	15-17	
	18-19	
	20-21	
	22-23	
	24-25	
	26-27	

UNIT OUTLINE – *Dracula*

1	2	3	4	5
Introduction: The 19th Century Gothic Genre "Dracula's Guest" PVR- Ch. 1-2	Study ?s Ch. 1-2 PVR- Ch. 3-4 Non-fiction work: 19th Century Ideas	Study ?s Ch. 3-4 Media Center Visit PVR- Ch. 5-6	Study ?s Ch. 5-6 PVR Ch. 7-8 Quiz 1-6 Fairy Tales Old and New	Study ?s Ch. 7-8 PVR Ch. 9-10 Stoker's Images
6	**7**	**8**	**9**	**10**
Study ?s Ch 9-10 PVR- Ch. 11-12 19th Century Presentations	Study ?s Ch. 11-12 Quiz Ch. 7-12 PVR- Ch. 13-14 Characterization Posters	Study ?s Ch. 13-14 PVR. Ch. 15-17 Conflict	Study ?s Ch. 15-17 PVR- Ch 18-19 Media Center Writing Assignment 1	Study ?s Ch. 18-19 Quiz Ch. 13-17 PVR- Ch. 20-21
11	**12**	**13**	**14**	**15**
Study ?s Ch. 20-21 Epitaphs PVR- Ch 22-23	Study ?s Ch. 22-23 Quiz Ch. 18-21 PVR- Ch 24-25	Study ?s Ch. 24-25 Conflict PVR- Ch 26-27	Study ?s Ch. 26-27 Quiz Ch. 22-27 Writing Assignment 2	Gothic Poetry
16	**17**	**18**	**19**	**20**
Vocabulary Work	Group Work: Extra Discussion Questions	Research Work: begin posters for authors project	In-Class Writing Assignment 3: Persuasion Piece	Peer Editing: Persuasion Piece Finish posters
21	**22**	**23**	**24**	
Research Presentations Day 1	Research Presentations Day 2	Review Materials Creative Writing Due	Unit Test	

Key: P = Preview Study Questions V = Vocabulary Work R= Read

STUDY GUIDE QUESTIONS

SHORT ANSWER STUDY GUIDE QUESTIONS - *Dracula*

Chapters 1-2:
1. What is the setting of the first part of the story?
2. What does Jonathan Harker find waiting for him when he arrives at the Golden Krone Hotel?
3. Why does the hotel landlady beg Jonathan not to continue his journey?
4. What does the landlady of the hotel give Jonathan Harker for protection against evil?
5. How does Jonathan Harker describe the driver that meets him at the Borgo Pass?
6. What does Jonathan find strange about his carriage ride to Castle Dracula?
7. During Jonathan Harker's ride to Castle Dracula what is "all so strange and uncanny that a dreadful fear came upon [him]?"
8. What is it about the caleche driver that seems to make the biggest impression on Jonathan Harker?
9. Describe the man who greets Jonathan Harker at Castle Dracula.
10. Who are the "children of the night?"
11. What does Jonathan Harker notice is absent from every room he enters in the castle?
12. What does the Count want Jonathan Harker to teach him while at Castle Dracula?
13. What is Jonathan Harker's occupation, and what is his purpose for coming to Transylvania?
14. When Jonathan Harker looks in his shaving mirror, what peculiar thing does he notice about the Count?
15. What surprises Jonathan Harker when he tries to explore the outdoor grounds of Castle Dracula?

Chapters 3-4:
1. Describe Jonathan Harker's thoughts after he discovers the Count laying the table in the dining room.
2. Count Dracula claims to be the ancestor of what famous warrior?
3. What does the Count warn Jonathan not to do when he is alone at night?
4. Describe the way Jonathan Harker sees the Count leave the Castle.
5. Jonathan Harker falls asleep in the parlor. What does he see upon waking?
6. Describe the Count's reaction to finding the women with Jonathan Harker.
7. What does Jonathan Harker believe he hears coming from the bag the Count had thrown to the floor?
8. What happens to the women and the bag?
9. The Count instructs Jonathan to write three letters home. What is the content of these letters?
10. Jonathan attempts to send letters home without the Count reading them. What happens to the letters?
11. What does Jonathan discover upon waking on 31 May?
12. What do the Slovaks deliver to the castle?
13. When Count Dracula leaves the castle on 24 June, what does Jonathan Harker notice?
14. Jonathan goes to the window when he hears the agonizing cry of a woman. What does she yell upon seeing Jonathan's face in the window?
15. What happens to the woman as she continues to bang on the door of the Count's castle?

Dracula Study Questions page 2

Chapters 3-4 continued:
16. Jonathan decides to climb the wall of the castle into the Count's room. Describe what Jonathan Harker discovers in the Count's room.
17. Jonathan tells the Count that he wants to leave the night of 29 June, but he suddenly changes his mind. Why?
18. What does Jonathan Harker find when he goes back to the Count's room to look for a key to the door?

Chapters 5-6:
1. What is the relationship between Mina Murry and Jonathan Harker?
2. What kind of an institution does Dr. John Seward run?
3. From whom did Lucy receive marriage proposals?
4. Identify Quincey Morris.
5. Which of the marriage proposals does Lucy accept?
6. Describe the patient who seems to be of most interest to Dr. Seward.
7. What does the old man that Mina and Lucy meet claim about the tombstones in the cemetery?
8. Describe Renfield's systematic way of collecting lives.
9. What unusual thing does Renfield eat? Why?
10. What odd, recent behavior of Lucy is disturbing to Mina?

Chapters 7-8:
1. Describe the mysterious schooner's entrance into the harbor.
2. What is discovered on board the mysterious schooner?
3. What is the name of the schooner, and where did she come from?
4. What is the only living thing on the ship?
5. According to the captain's addendum to the ship's log, what happened to the men on the ship?
6. Describe what the captain saw on the last night aboard ship.
7. What happens to the old man who had befriended Mina and Lucy?
8. On August 11th what does Mina discover when she awakens in the night?
9. What does Mina see in the moonlit churchyard when she goes looking for Lucy?
10. What is Mina most concerned about for Lucy's sake as they walk home from the churchyard?
11. What makes Mina think that she pricked Lucy accidentally with a safety pin?
12. On the night of August 13th what does Mina see outside the window?
13. On August 14th Mina and Lucy notice a dark figure seated alone in the cemetery just before sundown. What is it about his appearance that startles Mina?
14. On August 18th what change does Mina begin to notice in Lucy?
15. What news does Mina receive that makes her both joyful and anxious at the same time?
16. What changes are taking place in Renfield?
17. Describe Renfield's escape and return.

Dracula Study Questions page 3

Chapters 9-10:
1. How does Mina describe Jonathan in her letter to Lucy?
2. What request does Jonathan make of Mina regarding his notebook?
3. Where were Mina and Jonathan married?
4. What does Mina do with Jonathan's notebook?
5. What daily pattern has developed in Renfield since Dr. Seward confined him to a straight jacket and a padded room?
6. Describe Renfield's second escape and capture.
7. What begins happening to Lucy upon her return home to Hillingham?
8. Arthur Holmwood asks Dr. Seward to examine Lucy. What are Dr. Seward's finding regarding Lucy?
9. Describe Lucy's condition when Dr. Seward and Van Helsing visit her on September 7th.
10. What action does Van Helsing believe is necessary to keep Lucy alive?
11. Who arrives and offers to help in Van Helsing's first treatment of Lucy?
12. What specific instruction does Van Helsing give Dr. Seward regarding Lucy before he left for Amsterdam?
13. What does Van Helsing discover upon his return to Hillingham?
14. Who aids Van Helsing in the second transfusion to Lucy?
15. What is in the package that Van Helsing receives from abroad?

Chapters 11-12:
1. What does Mrs. Westenra tell Van Helsing that causes him to break down in tears?
2. Who volunteers his arm for Lucy's third blood transfusion?
3. What happens as soon as the zookeeper finished telling his tale to the reporter?
4. After he is attacked by Renfield, what act does Dr. Seward witness that "positively sickened" him?
5. Explain what happens to Lucy's mother.
6. Describe what Dr. Seward and Van Helsing see in Lucy's bedroom.
7. Who gives blood in Lucy's fourth transfusion?
8. What strange action does Lucy do just as she was falling asleep after the fourth transfusion?
9. Describe Renfield's reaction when some men remove several heavy boxes from Carfax.
10. Describe the alarming physical changes in Lucy Westenra.
11. What does Van Helsing do when Arthur attempts to kiss Lucy?
12. What does Lucy ask Van Helsing when she awakens from her trance-like stupor?
13. What ultimately becomes of Lucy Westenra?

Dracula Study Questions page 4

Chapters 13-14:
1. What do Dr. Seward and Van Helsing notice about Lucy's body when they go to pay their respects?
2. What does Van Helsing want to do with Lucy's body?
3. What happens when the maid sits by Lucy's body during the night?
4. Who is Lord Godalming?
5. What request does Van Helsing make of Arthur regarding the Westenra estate?
6. As Jonathan Harker walks down Piccadilly what does he see that causes him to suddenly go pale?
7. After Jonathan Harker's sudden relapse, what does Mina declare it is time for her to do?
8. What secret do Dr. Seward, Van Helsing, and Quincy Morris vow to keep from Arthur?
9. What strange occurrences begin taking place in Hampstead not long after Lucy's funeral?
10. What does Mina learn that upsets her terribly?
11. What does Mina plan to do with Jonathan's diary?
12. After reading Mina's letters to Lucy, Dr. Van Helsing requests a visit with Mina. What specific event does he ask Mina to share in detail?
13. What does Mina allow Van Helsing to read?
14. What change comes over Jonathan after reading Van Helsing's note about the diaries?
15. Name at least three of the unexplained mysteries of the natural world Van Helsing tells Dr. Seward to make him accept the cause of Lucy's death and the wounds on the children of Hampstead.
16. How does Van Helsing explain the bite marks found on the children of Hampstead Heath?

Chapters 15-17:
1. Where is the first place Dr. Seward and Van Helsing go in an attempt to prove Van Helsing's theories about Lucy are true?
2. What does Dr. Vincent believe made the marks on the children's throats?
3. What do Van Helsing and Dr. Seward find when they open Lucy's coffin?
4. What do Van Helsing and Dr. Seward do after exiting Lucy's tomb?
5. What do Van Helsing and Dr. Seward do with the child they find in the cemetery?
6. What do Dr. Seward and Van Helsing discover when they return to Lucy's tomb the following afternoon?
7. Why does Van Helsing hesitate to immediately do what needs to be done to Lucy's body in order to bring her soul peace?
8. How does Van Helsing intend to keep Lucy inside her tomb at night?
9. What news does Van Helsing share with Arthur and Quincey Morris?
10. What does Arthur unwillingly agree to do?
11. Dr. Seward, Van Helsing, Quincey Morris, and Arthur find Lucy's tomb empty. What do they see in the cemetery the same night?
12. Describe Arthur's reaction when Lucy speaks to him in the cemetery.
13. How does Van Helsing protect Arthur from Lucy's temptation?
14. According to Van Helsing, what do the Eastern Europeans call the Un-Dead?
15. Who strikes the blow that sets Lucy's soul free?

Dracula Study Questions page 5

Chapters 15-17 continued:
16. What happens to Lucy's body after the stake is driven through her heart?
17. When the men exit Lucy's tomb for the last time, what does each strongly swear to do?
18. What does Van Helsing find waiting for him when he returns to the hotel?
19. What does Van Helsing give to Dr. Seward before he leaves for Amsterdam?
20. Who does Dr. Seward encourage to stay at his home?
21. Dr. Seward keeps his own personal diary on phonograph. What does Mina intend to do with Dr. Seward's wax cylinders?
22. What is ironic about the discovery of the Count's possible hiding place?
23. Who does Dr. Seward realize may be strangely linked to Count Dracula?
24. In Whitby, Jonathan tracks down the location of the Count's fifty large boxes. Where are they located?
25. What happens that causes Arthur to swear that he would be a life-long brother to Mina Harker?

Chapters 18-19:
1. Mina asks Dr. Seward if she can see Renfield. What is Renfield's method of "tidying up" his cell before her visit?
2. What is Renfield's explanation for eating live flies and spiders?
3. List the powers that Van Helsing claims Count Dracula has as a nosferatu.
4. What does Van Helsing claim is the greatest danger that the men face as they attempt to destroy Dracula?
5. What limitations does Van Helsing say that a vampire has?
6. What does Quincey Morris claim he was shooting at when he broke the parlor window at Dr. Seward's home?
7. What does Van Helsing tell Mina about the quest to hunt down the Count?
8. What is Renfield's reaction when Dr. Seward tells him that he may not leave the asylum?
9. How does Van Helsing prepare Dr. Seward and the others to go to Carfax to find the Count?
10. What do Dr. Seward and the others notice the most as they enter the old chapel at Carfax?
11. When thousands of rats swarm the chapel, how are the men able to continue searching?
12. How many boxes were missing from Carfax of the original fifty boxes shipped from Transylvania to London?
13. What does Jonathan Harker notice about his wife when he returns from Carfax?
14. Describe Van Helsing's meeting with Renfield the morning after the visit to Carfax.
15. What is distressing Mina regarding her husband's visit to the Count's house?
16. Why does Mina wish she'd never gone to Whitby to visit Lucy?
17. What strange dream does Mina describe?

Dracula Study Questions page 6

Chapters 20-21:
1. Where are the 21 boxes missing from Carfax taken?
2. What change does Jonathan Harker notice about Mina?
3. Renfield says that he wants life from other beings, but he does not want something else. What is it he does not want?
4. Dr. Seward notices that twice Renfield stops himself before uttering a specific word. What word is it?
5. After Dr. Seward leaves Renfield, what does the doctor realize?
6. Who do the realtors at Mitchell, Sons, and Candy claim purchased the house in Piccadilly?
7. What does Dr. Seward hear coming from Renfield's room that alarms him?
8. The asylum attendant reports to Dr. Seward that Renfield has met with an accident. Describe Renfieds injuries.
9. What procedure does Van Helsing perform on Renfield?
10. What does Count Dracula promise Renfield in exchange for letting him into the asylum?
11. Why does Renfield become angry with the Count?
12. What does Renfield notice about Mina Harker?
13. Describe the encounter between Renfield and Dracula when the Count returns to the asylum.
14. Describe the scene Van Helsing, Dr. Seward, Lord Godalming, and Quincey Morris witness after breaking down the door to the Harkers' bedroom.
15. Upon escaping, what does the Count do with the typed manuscript and phonograph diary entries?
16. Recount Mina's description of her encounter with Dracula.

Chapters 22-23:
1. What do the men discover when they return to Renfield's room?
2. What decision do Dr. Seward and Van Helsing make regarding Mina's knowledge of their activities?
3. Mina vows to kill herself if she will endanger the others in any way. Why does Dr. Van Helsing tell her this can not be?
4. How does Van Helsing propose to enter the Count's locked house in Piccadilly by daylight without drawing unnecessary attention?
5. Why does Van Helsing say that the group will be unlikely to run into the Count during the day?
6. What happens as a result of Van Helsing's attempt to protect Mina from the Count while they are gone?
7. How does Van Helsing purify the boxes of earth at Carfax?
8. What are the men distressed to learn about the boxes of earth at the Piccadilly house?
9. What personal effects belonging to the Count do the men find at Piccadilly?
10. Describe the physical changes that have taken place in Jonathan Harker in the past twenty four hours.
11. What does Van Helsing learn of Count Dracula's mortal life?
12. What message is delivered to Van Helsing at the Piccadilly house?
13. Who is the first to attempt to attack the Count upon Dracula's arrival at Piccadilly?

Dracula Study Questions page 7

Chapters 22-23 continued:
14. How does the Count escape capture from the group at Piccadilly?
15. What does the Count desperately attempt to take with him as he escaped from the house?
16. What is the noise that Mina hears outside their bedroom in the night?
17. What request does Mina make of Van Helsing?
18. With what information is Mina able to supply Van Helsing?

Chapters 24-25:
1. Where does Van Helsing believe that the Count is going?
2. What news does the man from Doolittle's Wharf share with Van Helsing?
3. Why does the Czarina Catherine not sail out on time?
4. Why do Jonathan Harker and the others feel so compelled to follow the Count even though he is leaving the country?
5. Explain Van Helsing's comparison of Dracula to a tiger.
6. What is a constant reminder that the events surrounding Dracula are real and not a dream?
7. Why does Van Helsing propose to keep Mina in the dark about the group's plans for the Count?
8. What weapon does Quincey Morris suggest the group should add to their arsenal?
9. What request does Mina make regarding the group's journey to follow the Count?
10. What solemn promise does Mina ask of Jonathan Harker and the other men?
11. What does Mina ask Jonathan to read for her?
12. What does Mina claim to hear when Van Helsing puts her into a hypnotic trance?
13. Who is "Judge Money-bag" that Jonathan Harker refers to in his journal?
14. What news does Van Helsing and the others receive about the Czarina Catherine?
15. How did the Count find out that Van Helsing and the others were chasing him?
16. What makes Van Helsing so absolutely certain that the Count is returning to his castle in Transylvania?

Chapters 26-27:
1. What does Van Helsing learn from Mina in her hypnotic state?
2. What seems to be happening to Mina's hypnotic trances?
3. What had the Romanians on the crew of the Czarina Catherine requested several times of their captain?
4. What becomes of Petrof Skinsky who has claimed the Count's box from the ship?
5. What does Mina do for which Van Helsing and the others heartily congratulated her?
6. What single word does Mina hesitate to write in her journal?
7. How does the group divide its members in order to best capture the Count?
8. How does Lord Godalming manage to trick boat owners to allow him to search their vessels along the river?
9. What seems to arouse the superstitions of the people that Van Helsing and Mina meet along their journey?
10. Describe the changes in Mina's behavior since she and Van Helsing separated from the others.

Dracula Study Questions page 8

Chapters 26-27 continued:
11. What precaution does Van Helsing take when he and Mina are forced to sleep outside for the night?
12. What does Van Helsing see in the mist during the night?
13. Although Mina is safe from vampires inside her circle, what other danger concerns Van Helsing?
14. Van Helsing hesitates before killing the first vampire woman. What brings him back to his sense of purpose?
15. What happens to each of the female vampires once Van Helsing has purified them?
16. What does Van Helsing see through his field glass as he stood upon the large rock?
17. How is Count Dracula finally destroyed?
18. What becomes of the members of the group after their terrible ordeal?

ANSWER KEY SHORT ANSWER STUDY GUIDE QUESTIONS - *Dracula*

Chapter 1-2:

1. What is the setting of the first part of the story?
    It is set in Transylvania in the midst of the Carpathian Mountains.

2. What does Jonathan Harker find waiting for him when he arrives at the Golden Krone Hotel?
    There is a note from Count Dracula waiting for him that says his coachman will meet Jonathan at the Borgo Pass to bring him to Castle Dracula.

3. Why does the hotel landlady beg Jonathan not to continue his journey?
    She tells him it is the Eve of St. George's Day, and when the clock strikes midnight, all the evil things in the world will have full sway.

4. What does the landlady of the hotel give Jonathan Harker for protection against evil?
    When Jonathan refuses to cancel his trip to Castle Dracula, she gives him her crucifix for protection against evil.

5. How does Jonathan Harker describe the driver that meets him at the Borgo Pass?
    He is a tall man with a long brown beard and a great black hat, which seems to hide his face. Jonathan could see the gleam of a pair of very bright eyes which seemed red in the lamplight.

6. What does Jonathan find strange about his carriage ride to Castle Dracula?
    Jonathan feels they are traveling over and over the same ground. He then hears the howling of dogs, later followed by the howling of wolves. The wind increases and it becomes colder. Jonathan also seese a faint flickering blue flame.

7. During Jonathan Harker's ride to Castle Dracula what is "all so strange and uncanny that a dreadful fear came upon [him]"?
    The driver raises his arms and seems to command the wolves to silence. When the wolves do stop their howling, Jonathan is afraid.

8. What is it about the caleche driver that seems to make the biggest impression on Jonathan Harker?
    Jonathan cannot help but marvel at the man's great strength.

9. Describe the man who greets Jonathan Harker at Castle Dracula.
    He is a tall old man, clean shaven save for a long white moustache. He is dressed in black without a speck of color anywhere.

10. Who are the "children of the night?"
    The wolves that are howling outside the castle at night are the "children of the night."

11. What does Jonathan Harker notice is absent from every room he enters in the castle?
    He notices that there are no mirrors in the castle.

12. What does the Count want Jonathan Harker to teach him while at Castle Dracula?
    The Count wants Jonathan Harker to teach him to speak English well enough that he would never be recognized as a foreigner.

13. What is Jonathan Harker's occupation, and what is his purpose for coming to Transylvania?
    Jonathan Harker is an attorney who has come to Transylvania to close a real estate transaction for a house in England that the Count purchased.

14. When Jonathan Harker looks in his shaving mirror, what peculiar thing does he notice about the Count?
    The Count casts no reflection in Jonathan's shaving mirror.

15. What surprises Jonathan Harker when he tries to explore the outdoor grounds of Castle Dracula?
    All of the doors of the castle are locked, and he cannot get out.

Chapter 3-4:

1. Describe Jonathan Harker's thoughts after he discovers the Count laying the table in the dining room.
    Jonathan is sure there is no one else in the castle if the Count is performing menial tasks. He believes the Count was the driver who brought him to the castle. Being alone in the castle with the Count frightens him.

2. Count Dracula claims to be the ancestor of what famous warrior?
    He claims to be descended from Attila the Hun.

3. What does the Count warn Jonathan not to do when he is alone at night?
    The Count warns Jonathan against falling asleep in any part of the castle other than the areas that have been designated to him.

4. Describe the way Jonathan Harker sees the Count leave the Castle.
    Jonathan sees the Count crawl out a window, face down with his cloak spreading out around him like great wings. Jonathan watches as the Count moves down the wall like a lizard.

5. Jonathan Harker falls asleep in the parlor. What does he see upon waking?
    Jonathan sees three beautiful, voluptuous women with long sharp teeth, who try to seduce him.

6. Describe the Count's reaction to finding the women with Jonathan Harker.
    The Count is angry with the women, and he flings them violently aside. He tells them that Jonathan belongs to him first.

7. What does Jonathan Harker believe he hears coming from the bag the Count had thrown to the floor?
   Jonathan hears a gasp and a low wail, as of a half-smothered child.

8. What happens to the women and the bag?
   The women and the bag disappear; they seemed to fade into the rays of moonlight and pass out through the window.

9. The Count instructs Jonathan to write three letters home. What is the content of these letters?
   He is instructed to write one saying that his work in Transylvania is nearly done and that he will be leaving for home in a few days, a second saying that he would be leaving the castle the next morning from the time of the letter, and a third saying that he had left the castle and has arrived at Bistritz.

10. Jonathan attempts to send letters home without the Count reading them. What happens to the letters?
    Count Dracula intercepts the letters. After opening them, he decides to post the letter to Jonathan Harker's employer, but since the other (to Mina) was written in shorthand and the Count could not read it, the Count burned it.

11. What does Jonathan discover upon waking on 31 May?
    He discovers that all of his personal papers and his traveling clothes have disappeared from the closet.

12. What do the Slovaks deliver to the castle?
    They deliver empty large wooden boxes with rope handles and stack them outside the castle.

13. When Count Dracula leaves the castle on 24 June, what does Jonathan Harker notice?
    The Count is wearing Jonathan Harker's traveling clothes, and the terrible bag which Jonathan had seen the women take away is slung over his shoulder.

14. Jonathan goes to the window when he hears the agonizing cry of a woman. What does she yell upon seeing Jonathan's face in the window?
    "Monster! Give me back my child!"

15. What happens to the woman as she continues to bang on the door of the Count's castle?
    A pack of wolves arrive and tear her to pieces.

16. Jonathan decides to climb the wall of the castle into the Count's room. Describe what Jonathan Harker discovers in the Count's room.

The room is barely furnished with odd things, which seem to have never been used. In the corner is an unlocked heavy door that leads to an old, ruined chapel, which had evidently been a graveyard. The wooden boxes that had been delivered were filled with earth, and the Count was in a box on top of one of the piles of freshly dug earth. The Count's eyes were open, but they did not seem to register Jonathan's presence.

17. Jonathan tells the Count that he wants to leave the night of 29 June, but he suddenly changes his mind. Why?
    The Count tells Jonathan that he can leave if he wishes, and he opens the door. Just outside the door is a pack of snarling wolves ready to attack, so Jonathan begs the Count to close the door.

18. What does Jonathan Harker find when he goes back to the Count's room to look for a key to the door?
    He finds the Count inside a covered wooden box. When he removes the lid, Jonathan notices that the Count looks much younger and his body seems to be bloated with fresh blood.

Chapter 5-6:

1. What is the relationship between Mina Murray and Jonathan Harker?
   They are engaged to be married.

2. What kind of institution does Dr. John Seward run?
   He runs an insane asylum.

3. From whom did Lucy receive marriage proposals?
   Lucy received three marriage proposals in one day from Dr. John Seward, Mr. Quincey Morris, and Mr. Arthur Holmwood.

4. Identify Quincey Morris.
   Quincey Morris is an American friend of Arthur Holmwood. They go hunting together.

5. Which of the marriage proposals does Lucy accept?
   Lucy accepts Arthur Holmwood's proposal.

6. Describe the patient who seems to be of most interest to Dr. Seward.
   R. M. Renfield is about 59 years old, is very strong and extremely excitable. Dr. Seward thinks that he could be very dangerous.

7. What does the old man that Mina and Lucy meet claim about the tombstones in the cemetery?
   The old man claims that the tombstones lie about those who are buried (or supposedly are buried) in the graves.

8. Describe Renfield's systematic way of collecting lives.
    Renfield believes that one spider that eats many flies contains many lives. The bird that eats spiders that have eaten flies contains more lives. He who eats the bird ingests all of those lives.

9. What unusual thing does Renfield eat? Why?
    He eats flies, spiders, and birds to acquire their life blood so he'll live longer.

10. What odd, recent behavior of Lucy is disturbing to Mina?
    Lucy has begun sleepwalking.

Chapter 7-8:

1. Describe the mysterious schooner's entrance into the harbor.
    The schooner had full sails up in the storm. It was literally blown in by the high winds and it somehow maneuvered around dangerous rocks that had destroyed others ships in the past.

2. What is discovered on board the mysterious schooner?
    The body of the captain of the schooner is tied to the wheel of the ship. An addendum to the ship's log is found in his pocket.

3. What is the name of the schooner, and where does she come from?
    The ship, named the Demeter, is Russian and from Varna.

4. What is the only living thing on the ship?
    A large dog sprang up on deck from below and jumped to the sand, disappearing in the dark.

5. According to the captain's addendum to the ship's log, what happened to the men on the ship?
    Men on the ship mysteriously disappeared one by one.

6. Describe what the captain saw on the last night aboard ship.
    According to the captain's addendum, the captain witnessed the first mate come running (like a madman) from below deck, screaming that he would not allow whatever was below to take him. The first mate threw himself into the sea before the captain could stop him. The captain realized that he was the last man alive on the ship, and he refused to leave the helm. He tied himself to the wheel with a rosary in his hand.

7. What happens to the old man who had befriended Mina and Lucy?
    The old man is found dead in the cemetery where he used to visit with Mina and Lucy. His neck is broken.

8. On August 11th what does Mina discover when she awakens in the night?
    Lucy is not in her bed.

9. What does Mina see in the moonlit churchyard when she goes looking for Lucy?
    Mina sees a dark, sinister figure bent over Lucy in the churchyard.

10. What is Mina most concerned about for Lucy's sake as they walk home from the churchyard?
    Mina is concerned that Lucy will get sick from exposure to the night air, and that Lucy's reputation would be in jeopardy if anyone were to find out that she had been outdoors in nothing but her night dress.

11. What makes Mina think that she pricked Lucy accidentally with a safety pin?
    Mina notices two marks, like small holes, on Lucy's neck.

12. On the night of August 13th what does Mina see outside the window?
    Between Mina and the moonlight flitted a great bat, coming and going in great whirling circles.

13. On August 14th Mina and Lucy notice a dark figure seated alone in the cemetery just before sundown. What is it about his appearance that startles Mina?
    Mina is startled because it seemed for an instant as if the stranger had great eyes like buring flames.

14. On August 18th what change does Mina begin to notice in Lucy?
    After being so ill for a few days, Mina is pleased to notice that Lucy seems to be getting better in spite of still being "sadly pale and wan-looking."

15. What news does Mina receive that makes her both joyful and anxious at the same time?
    Mina finally hears news of her fiancé Jonathan Harker, but she learns that he is terribly ill.

16. What changes are taking place in Renfield?
    The attendant notices that he has began to get excited and to sniff around his cell like a dog. He also has assumed a haughty air and has exclaimed that "the Master is at hand."

17. Describe Renfield's escape and return.
    Someone or something wrenched Renfield's window from the wall, and he climbed out through it. He was found at the neighboring Carfax estate pressed against the chapel door, talking to someone on the other side saying, "I am here to do Your bidding, Master." He was finally captured after putting up a terrible fight and, after being returned to the hospital, he was put in a straight jacket and chained to a wall in a padded room.

Chapter 9-10:

1. How does Mina describe Jonathan in her letter to Lucy?
    He is "thin, pale, and weak-looking. All the resolution has gone out of... his eyes... he is only a wreck of himself, and he does not remember anything that has happened to him for a long time past."

2. What request does Jonathan make of Mina regarding his notebook?
    He tells her to keep the notebook and read it if she wants to, but she must never tell him what is on the pages unless some extreme emergency were to arise that would force him to look back on what had happened.

3. Where are Mina and Jonathan married?
    Mina and Jonathan were married at the hospital.

4. What does Mina do with Jonathan's notebook?
    She wraps the book in white paper and ties it with a blue ribbon. She uses her wedding ring to seal the knot with wax and tells Jonathan that she will never break the seal unless it were for his sake or "for the sake of some solemn duty."

5. What daily pattern has developed in Renfield since Dr. Seward confined him to a straight jacket and a padded room?
    He has become violent during the day, and he is "quiet from moonrise to sunrise."

6. Describe Renfield's second escape and capture.
    Renfield hid behind the door as the attendant entered the cell to check on him, and he ran out the door. Once again, he ran to Carfax and was extremely violent as the attendant tried to capture him. Suddenly, he became very calm and allowed himself to be taken peacefully. At this point, Dr. Seward followed Renfield's gaze and noticed a giant bat flying away.

7. What begins happening to Lucy upon her return home to Hillingham?
    She has begun having nightmares like she did in Whitby, and she is terribly frightened. She also feels very weak and worn out. Her throat is sore, and she is very pale. She also cannot seem to get enough air.

8. Arthur Holmwood asks Dr. Seward to examine Lucy. What are Dr. Seward's findings regarding Lucy?
    He cannot find "any functional disturbance or any malady" that he is familiar with. Even though he can find nothing "wrong," he is concerned about her appearance and her weakness.

9. Describe Lucy's condition when Dr. Seward and Van Helsing visit her on September 7th.
    *Lucy "was ghastly, chalkily pale; the red seemed to have gone even
    from her lips and gums, and the bones of her face stood out prominently."
    She was also having a difficult time breathing.*

10. What action does Van Helsing believe is necessary to keep Lucy alive?
    *Van Helsing believes that Lucy needs an immediate blood transfusion to
    save her life.*

11. Who arrives and offers to help in Van Helsing's first treatment of Lucy?
    *Arthur Holmwood, Lucy's fiancé, arrives and allows his blood to
    be given to Lucy.*

12. What specific instructions does Van Helsing give Dr. Seward regarding Lucy before he left for Amsterdam?
    *Van Helsing instructs Dr. Seward to sit up with Lucy through the
    night and not to leave her unguarded.*

13. What does Van Helsing discover upon his return to Hillingham?
    *Dr. Van Helsing found Dr. Seward asleep. When they checked Lucy, they found
    her more horribly white and wan-looking than ever.*

14. Who aids Van Helsing in the second transfusion to Lucy?
    Dr. Seward allows his blood to be transfused into Lucy.

15. What is in the package that Van Helsing receives from abroad?
    The box is filled with garlic flowers.

Chapter 11-12:

1. What does Mrs. Westenra tell Van Helsing that causes him to break down in tears?
    *Mrs. Westenra tells Van Helsing that she had opened the windows
    in Lucy's stuffy room and had thrown out the horrible smelling flowers.*

2. Who volunteers his arm for Lucy's third blood transfusion?
    Dr. Van Helsing offers his blood.

3. What happens as soon as the zookeeper finished telling his tale to the reporter?
    *The moment the zookeeper finishes telling the tale about the escaped wolf,
    the wolf returns peacefully.*

4. After he is attacked by Renfield, what act does Dr. Seward witness that "positively sickened" him?
    Renfield is lapping the doctor's blood off the floor like a dog.

5. Describe what happens to Lucy's mother.
   Mrs. Westenra goes to Lucy's room to see if she is all right. Lucy asks her to come in and sleep with her. Later she is startled by a sound at the window and a low howl in the shrubbery, followed by a grey wolf breaking in the window. Mrs. Westenra is terrified and dies of heart failure.

6. Describe what Dr. Seward and Van Helsing see in Lucy's bedroom.
   They find Lucy and her mother lying in Lucy's bed. Mrs. Westenra is dead, and Lucy is near death. The flowers that Van Helsing had placed around Lucy's neck are upon Mrs. Westenra's bosom, and the marks on Lucy's throat are worse than ever before.

7. Who gives blood in Lucy's fourth transfusion?
   Lucy receives blood from Quincey Morris.

8. What strange action does Lucy do just as she is falling asleep after the fourth transfusion?
   She begins to tear the note she'd written to pieces. When Vann Helsing takes the pieces from her hands, she continues to pantomime the tearing of the papers.

9. Describe Renfield's reaction when some men remove several heavy boxes from Carfax.
   He attacks them.

10. Describe the alarming physical changes in Lucy Westenra.
    She has become increasingly pale, and her teeth have become longer and sharper.

11. What does Van Helsing do when Arthur attempts to kiss Lucy?
    He pulls Arthur away violently and throws him across the room away from her.

12. What does Lucy ask Van Helsing when she awakens from her trance-like stupor?
    She asks him to guard Arthur and give her peace.

13. What ultimately becomes of Lucy Westenra?
    She dies.

Chapter 13-14:

1. What do Dr. Seward and Van Helsing notice about Lucy's body when they go to pay their respects?
   Lucy looks more beautiful in death, and she seems very life-like.

2. What does Van Helsing want to do with Lucy's body?
   He wants to perform an operation to cut off her head and take out her heart.

3. What happens when the maid sits by Lucy's body during the night?
   She steals the gold crucifix that Van Helsing had placed on Lucy's body.

4. Who is Lord Godalming?
   Lord Godalming is Arthur Holmwood's new title after the death of his father.

5. What request does Van Helsing make of Arthur regarding the Westenra estate?
   He wants to be able to read through Lucy's letters and diary.

6. As Jonathan Harker walks down Piccadilly what does he see that causes him to suddenly go pale?
   He sees Count Dracula, but the Count looks younger.

7. After Jonathan Harker's sudden relapse, what does Mina declare it is time for her to do?
   She decides to read Jonathan's diary from when he was in Transylvania.

8. What secret do Dr. Seward, Van Helsing, and Quincy Morris vow to keep from Arthur?
   Since Arthur believes that the transfusion he gave Lucy makes them truly married in his eyes, Van Helsing and the others vow to never let him know that they also gave her blood transfusions.

9. What strange occurrences begin taking place in Hampstead not long after Lucy's funeral?
   Children are mysteriously disappearing and later reappearing, claiming that they were playing with a "bloofer lady."

10. What does Mina learn that upsets her terribly?
    She reads Jonathan's diary from when he was in Transylvania, and she knows of the terrible ordeal he went through.

11. What does Mina plan to do with Jonathan's diary?
    She is going to type it up so that others may read it and learn about the Count.

12. After reading Mina's letters to Lucy, Dr. Van Helsing requests a visit with Mina. What specific event does he ask Mina to share in detail?
    Van Helsing wants to know more about the night that Lucy was sleepwalking in the cemetery in Whitby.

13. What does Mina allow Van Helsing to read?
    Mina gives Van Helsing both her diary and Jonathan's to read.

14. What change comes over Jonathan after reading Van Helsing's note about the diaries?
    He becomes suddenly stronger and more self-assured because he no longer doubts himself about what happened with the Count.

15. Name at least three of the unexplained mysteries of the natural world Van Helsing tells Dr. Seward to make him accept the cause of Lucy's death and the wounds on the children of Hampstead.

Van Helsing's tells him that history is filled with events that have been unexplainable, yet true. He holds that faith "enables us to believe things which we know to be untrue." Examples are:
a. There are bats that exist that drain the blood of cattle and horses
b. Tortoises, elephants and parrots live longer than generations of men
c. Toads sealed inside rocks for thousands of years still lived
d. The Indian fakir can rise from the dead after several years

16. How does Van Helsing explain the bite marks found on the children of Hampstead Heath?
    He claims that Lucy made the bite marks on the children's throats.

Chapter 15-17:

1. Where is the first place Dr. Seward and Van Helsing go in an attempt to prove Van Helsing's heories about Lucy are true?
   They go to the hospital in Hampstead to see the bitten children.

2. What does Dr. Vincent believe made the marks on the children's throats?
   Dr. Vincent believes that bats made the marks on the children's throats.

3. What do Van Helsing and Dr. Seward find when they open Lucy's coffin?
   Lucy is not in the coffin.

4. What do Van Helsing and Dr. Seward do after exiting Lucy's tomb?
   They hide in the trees to watch the activity in the cemetery.

5. What do Van Helsing and Dr. Seward do with the child they find in the cemetery?
   They leave the child where a police officer could easily find it and return it to its parents.

6. What do Dr. Seward and Van Helsing discover when they return to Lucy's tomb the following afternoon?
   Lucy is in her coffin, and she looks more beautiful than ever.

7. Why does Van Helsing hesitate to immediately do what needs to be done to Lucy's body in order to bring her soul peace?
   Van Helsing believes that Arthur should know the truth about the circumstances surrounding Lucy's death.

8. How does Van Helsing intend to keep Lucy inside her tomb at night?
   Van Helsing places garlic and a crucifix in the tomb so that Lucy will not get out.

9. What news does Van Helsing share with Arthur and Quincey Morris?
   Van Helsing tells them that Lucy is one of the Un-Dead.

10. What does Arthur unwillingly agree to do?
    Arthur unwillingly agrees to visit Lucy's tomb with Van Helsing.

11. Dr. Seward, Van Helsing, Quincey Morris, and Arthur find Lucy's tomb empty. What do they see in the cemetery the same night?
    They see Lucy in her vampire form, and they witness her attack of a child.

12. Describe Arthur's reaction when Lucy speaks to him in the cemetery.
    Arthur is mesmerized, and he moves towards her as if in a trance.

13. How does Van Helsing protect Arthur from Lucy's temptation?
    Van Helsing jumps between Lucy and Arthur, and he holds up a crucifix towards Lucy.

14. According to Van Helsing, what do the Eastern Europeans call the Un-Dead?
    They call the Un-Dead "Nosferatu."

15. Who strikes the blow that sets Lucy's soul free?
    Arthur Holmwood (Lord Godalming) pounds a stake through Lucy's heart.

16. What happens to Lucy after the stake is driven through her heart?
    She no longer looks like a vile creature; she is the beautiful, sweet Lucy that the men had known.

17. When the men exit Lucy's tomb for the last time, what does each strongly swear to do?
    Each of the men is determined to find Count Dracula and destroy him.

18. What does Van Helsing find waiting for him when he returns to the hotel?
    Mina has sent a telegram saying that she is on her way to meet with Van Helsing.

19. What does Van Helsing give to Dr. Seward before he leaves for Amsterdam?
    Van Helsing gives Dr. Seward the Harker's journals to read so that he may know all.

20. Who does Dr. Seward encourage to stay at his home?
    He invites Mina Harker to stay as his guest while she is in town.

21. Dr. Seward keeps his own personal diary on phonograph. What does Mina intend to do with Dr. Seward's wax cylinders?
    Mina intends to transcribe his diary with her typewriter.

22. What is ironic about the discovery of the Count's possible hiding place?
    Count Dracula owns Carfax which is right next door to Dr. Seward.

23. Who does Dr. Seward realize may be strangely linked to Count Dracula?
    Dr. Seward believes that Renfield may be somehow in league with the Count.

24. In Whitby Jonathan tracks down the location of the Count's fifty large boxes. Where are they located?
    The fifty boxes had been delivered to Carfax.

25. What happens that causes Arthur to swear that he would be a life-long brother to Mina Harker?
    Mina comforts him over the death of Lucy.

Chapter 18-19:

1. Mina asks Dr. Seward if she can see Renfield. What is Renfield's method of "tidying up" cell before her visit?
   He eats all of the flies and the spiders he had captured.

2. What is Renfield's explanation for eating live flies and spiders?
   He claims that the blood of the insects would bring him an indefinitely prolonged life.

3. List the powers that Van Helsing claims Count Dracula has as a nosferatu.
   Van Helsing claims that Dracula can be a shape-shifter (into a mist or an animal), has power over weather, and has eternal life.

4. What does Van Helsing claim is the greatest danger that the men face as they attempt to destroy Dracula?
   The greatest danger is that they would become vampires themselves.

5. What limitations does Van Helsing say a vampire has?
   a. *no food but blood*
   b. *no shadow or reflection*
   c. *cannot enter a place unless invited to do so*
   d. *no daytime powers*
   e. *cannot pass over running water except at high and low tides*
   f. *repulsed by garlic and sacred objects (crucifixes, the Host, etc)*

6. What does Quincey Morris claim he was shooting at when he broke the parlor window at Dr. Seward's home?
   Quincey Morris claims that there was a large bat sitting on the windowsill.

7. What does Van Helsing tell Mina about the quest to hunt down the Count?
   Van Helsing tells Mina that she can no longer be involved because it is too dangerous for her.

8. What is Renfield's reaction when Dr. Seward tells him that he may not leave the asylum?
   Renfield becomes hysterical, and he begs to be allowed to leave under any condition.

9. How does Van Helsing prepare Dr. Seward and the others to go to Carfax to find the Count?
    *He gives them "weapons" against the Count: crucifixes, a gun, knives,
    and the Host (consecrated communion wafers).*

10. What do Dr. Seward and the others notice the most as they enter the old chapel at Carfax?
    The putrid smell is almost unbearable.

11. When thousands of rats swarm the chapel, how are the men able to continue searching?
    *Arthur summoned nearby dogs with a silver dog whistle, and the dogs
    drove the rats away.*

12. How many boxes were missing from Carfax of the original fifty boxes shipped from Transylvania to London?
    Twenty-one boxes were unaccounted for from the original fifty.

13. What does Jonathan Harker notice about his wife when he returns from Carfax?
    She is sleeping very deeply and looks deathly pale.

14. Describe Van Helsing's meeting with Renfield the morning after the visit to Carfax.
    Renfield has become sullen, and he calls Van Helsing an "old fool."

15. What is distressing Mina regarding her husband's visit to the Count's house?
    *She is being kept in the dark about what has been happening in order
    to protect her.*

16. Why does Mina wish she'd never gone to Whitby to visit Lucy?
    *Mina feels responsible for Lucy's sleepwalking, and if Mina had not
    come to Whitby, Lucy would not have been destroyed by Count Dracula.*

17. What strange dream does Mina describe?
    She sees gleaming red eyes through a mist.

Chapter 20-21:

1. Where are the twenty-one boxes missing from Carfax taken?
    *Six boxes where taken to Mile End New Town, another six boxes to Jamaica
    Lane in Bermondsey (both are in east London), and nine of the boxes were taken
    to Piccadilly (central London).*

2. What changes does Jonathan Harker notice about Mina?
    Mina is extremely pale, tired, and she shudders at the mention of Dracula.

3. Renfield says that he wants life from other beings, but he does not want something else. What is it he does not want?
    He does not want souls.

4. Dr. Seward notices that twice Renfield stops himself before uttering a specific word. What word is it?
   Renfield stops himself before he uttering the word "drink."

5. After Dr. Seward leaves Renfield, what does the doctor realize?
   Dr. Seward realizes that the Count has had contact with Renfield.

6. Who do the realtors at Mitchell, Sons, and Candy claim purchased the house in Piccadilly?
   They say that Count de Ville bought the house.

7. What does Dr. Seward hear coming from Renfield's room that alarms him?
   Dr. Seward hears a blood-curdling scream.

8. The asylum attendant reports to Dr. Seward that Renfield has met with an accident. Describe Renfieds injuries.
   Renfield's face has been smashed against the floor, and his back is broken.

9. What procedure does Van Helsing perform on Renfield?
   Van Helsing attempts to remove pressure from the brain by removing a part of Renfield's skull.

10. What does Count Dracula promise Renfield in exchange for letting him into the asylum?
    Dracula promises him the lives of rats.

11. Why does Renfield become angry with the Count?
    Renfield realizes that Dracula only promised him lives just to gain entrance to the asylum to get to Mina. The Count has lied and gives Renfield nothing.

12. What does Renfield notice about Mina Harker?
    He notices how pale she is and realizes the Count has taken her blood.

13. Describe the encounter between Renfield and Dracula when the Count returns to the asylum.
    Renfield attacks the Count to keep him from going back to Mina, but the Count smashes Renfield's face into the floor and breaks his back.

14. Describe the scene Van Helsing, Dr. Seward, Lord Godalming, and Quincey Morris witness after breaking down the door to the Harkers' bedroom.
    Jonathan Harker is in a sound, drug-like sleep, and Mina is in a trance. The Count is standing over Mina, forcing her to drink his blood from an open wound in his chest.

15. Upon escaping, what does the Count do with the typed manuscript and phonograph diary entries?
    He throws them into the fire.

16. Recount Mina's description of her encounter with Dracula.
    She and Jonathan had both been asleep when she awoke to find a mysterious mist in the room. When the mist dissipated, a man in black seemed to emerge from it. He threatened Jonathan's life if Mina did not do his bidding. The man in black then drank Mina's blood from her throat. He then used his sharp fingernail to open a vein in his chest, and he forced Mina's face to the wound to make her drink his blood.

Chapter 22-23:

1. What do the men discover when they return to Renfield's room?
    Renfield is dead. His face is completely smashed, and his neck is broken.

2. What decision does Dr. Seward and Van Helsing make regarding Mina's knowledge of their activities?
    They decide it is best to take Mina into full confidence.

3. Mina vows to kill herself if she will endanger the others in any way. Why does Dr. Van Helsing tell her this can not be?
    Dr. Van Helsing tells her she must not die before the Count because she would become like him.

4. How does Van Helsing propose to enter the Count's locked house in Piccadilly by daylight without drawing unnecessary attention?
    Lord Godalming and Quincey Morris will hire a locksmith and pretend that they lost the key to the house. Since they will be doing this in broad daylight, no one will question their behavior.

5. Why does Van Helsing say that the group will be unlikely to run into the Count during the day?
    The Count fed heavily (on Mina) the night before.

6. What happens as a result of Van Helsing's attempt to protect Mina from the Count while they are gone?
    Van Helsing tries to protect Mina by placing a piece of the Host on her forehead. Instead of protecting her, it burns into her skin, leaving a nasty scar.

7. How does Van Helsing purify the boxes of earth at Carfax?
    He places a piece of the Host in each one.

8. What are the men distressed to learn about the boxes of earth at the Piccadilly house?
   There had been nine boxes delivered to the house in Piccadilly, but there are only eight of them there.

9. What personal effects belonging to the Count do the men find at Piccadilly?
   They find deeds to the various properties that the Count has acquired, keys to the houses, writing materials, and personal hygiene items, one of them a basin of dirty water that is "reddened as if with blood."

10. Describe the physical changes that have taken place in Jonathan Harker in the past twenty-four hours.
    He has gone from a strong, youthful man full of energy with dark brown hair to a drawn, haggard old man with white hair, hollow eyes, and a grief-lined face.

11. What does Van Helsing learn of Count Dracula's mortal life?
    He had been a soldier, statesman, and a brilliant alchemist. He had a mighty brain, a learning beyond compare, and a heart that knew no fear or remorse. He also apparently attended Scholomance, a mythical school of dark magic.

12. What message is delivered to Van Helsing at the Piccadilly house?
    Mina sends a telegram warning them that she saw Dracula leave quickly from Carfax and that he may be looking for them.

13. Who is the first to attempt to attack the Count upon Dracula's arrival at Piccadilly?
    Jonathan Harker tries to stab Dracula with his Kukri knife.

14. How does the Count escape capture from the group at Piccadilly?
    He jumps out the window.

15. What does the Count desperately attempt to take with him as he escaped from the house?
    He grabs as many gold coins as he could carry.

16. What is the noise that Mina hears outside their bedroom in the night?
    She hears Quincey Morris who has brought his mattress into the hallway outside the Harkers' bedroom so that he can watch over them.

17. What request does Mina make of Van Helsing?
    She wants Van Helsing to hypnotize her because she believes that she can provide information about the Count's activities. Since she has taken his blood, there is a telepathic link between them.

18. With what information is Mina able to supply Van Helsing?
    She is able to describe sounds that lead Van Helsing to believe that Dracula is on a boat somewhere.

Chapter 24-25:

1. Where does Van Helsing believe that the Count is going?
    He believes that the Count is going home to Transylvania.

2. What news does the man from Doolittle's Wharf share with Van Helsing?
    The man tells Van Helsing that a tall, thin, pale man with a high nose and white teeth with burning eyes booked passage across the Black Sea. The man brought a giant box on board with him.

3. Why does the Czarina Catherine not sail out on time?
    A sudden dense fog held up the departure. Dracula created the fog so that he could board the ship at the change of the tide.

4. Why do Jonathan Harker and the others feel so compelled to follow the Count even though he is leaving the country?
    They believe that the Count must be destroyed not only for Mina's sake, but for the sake of humanity.

5. Explain Van Helsing's comparison of Dracula to a tiger.
    A tiger is a flesh eater who never ceases to be proud. Once it has tasted human flesh, there is no going back. The same could be said for Count Dracula and his thirst for human blood.

6. What is a constant reminder that the events surrounding Dracula are real and not a dream?
    The scar on Mina's forehead is a constant reminder that Dracula is real.

7. Why does Van Helsing propose to keep Mina in the dark about the group's plans for the Count?
    Van Helsing is afraid that Dracula can read Mina's mind and will know what the group is up to.

8. What weapon does Quincey Morris suggest the group add to their arsenal?
    He suggests the use of Winchester rifles against the wolves.

9. What request does Mina make regarding the group's journey to follow the Count?
    She will go with them to capture the Count.

10. What solemn promise does Mina ask of Jonathan Harker and the other men?
    She makes the men promise that if they see her change for the worse that they will kill her and free her soul just as they did for Lucy.

11. What does Mina ask Jonathan to read for her?
    She asks him to read the Burial Service of the Dead.

12. What does Mina claim to hear when Van Helsing puts her into a hypnotic trance?
    She hears nothing at first, but then only the sound of waves lapping against the ship.

13. Who is "Judge Money-bag" that Jonathan Harker refers to in his journal?
    It is bribery money that they will use to get on to the ship.

14. What news do Van Helsing and the others receive about the Czarina Catherine?
    The Czarina Catherine ported at Galatz instead of at Varna. The Count is attempting to escape capture.

15. How does the Count find out that Van Helsing and the others were chasing him?
    The Count's mind is linked to Mina's.

16. What makes Van Helsing so absolutely certain that the Count is returning to his castle in Transylvania?
    In the past, the Count had returned there after an attack in Turkey. When things went wrong, he pulled back to his home to regroup.

Chapter 26-27:

1. What does Van Helsing learn from Mina in her hypnotic state?
    She tells Van Helsing she hears oars being lifted in and out of the water, there is a gleam of light, and she can feel air blowing upon her.

2. What seems to be happening to Mina's hypnotic trances?
    It is becoming more and more difficult for Van Helsing to hypnotize her.

3. What had the Romanians on the crew of the Czarina Catherine requested several times of their captain?
    The superstitious Romanians wanted to cast the giant box they were carrying overboard into the sea.

4. What becomes of Petrof Skinsky who has claimed the Count's box from the ship?
    He is found inside a churchyard with his throat torn open.

5. What does Mina do for which Van Helsing and the others heartily congratulated her?
    She logically figures out the route the Count must be taking to get back to his castle.

6. What single word does Mina hesitate to write in her journal?
    Mina can not bring herself to write the word "vampire" in her journal.

7. How does the group divide its members in order to best capture the Count?
    Arthur and Jonathan will take a steamboat and attempt to locate the boat that Dracula is on. Dr. Seward and Quincey Morris will travel along the riverbank on horseback to make sure the Count doesn't get on land. Mina and Van Helsing will go directly to Castle Dracula to destroy his lair.

8. How does Lord Godalming manage to trick boat owners to allow him to search their vessels along the river?
    He flies a Rumanian flag on the steamboat, and the people on the other boats think he is a government official searching their boats.

9. What seems to arouse the superstitions of the people that Van Helsing and Mina meet along their journey?
    They see the scar on Mina's forehead and take it for a bad omen.

10. Describe the changes in Mina's behavior since she and Van Helsing separated from the others.
    Mina has begun sleeping more during the day, she no longer writes in her journal, and she seems to know how to get to Castle Dracula by instinct.

11. What precaution does Van Helsing take when he and Mina are forced to sleep outside for the night?
    Van Helsing draws a circle around her, and he uses the Host to create a boundary to both keep her in the circle and to keep other vampires out.

12. What does Van Helsing see in the mist during the night?
    He sees three beautiful women.

13. Although Mina is safe from vampires inside her circle, what other danger concerns Van Helsing?
    Van Helsing hears wolves howling nearby.

14. Van Helsing hesitates before killing the first vampire woman. What brings him back to his sense of purpose?
    He hesitates because he is momentarily hypnotized by her beauty, but when he hears Mina wailing, he kills the vampire.

15. What happens to each of the female vampires once Van Helsing has purified them?
    They all turn to dust.

16. What does Van Helsing see through his field glass as he stood upon the large rock?
    He sees an approaching carriage carrying a huge chest.
    Other men are fast approaching the carriage on horseback.

17. How is Count Dracula finally destroyed?
    Jonathan Harker slits the Count's throat with his Kukri knife, and
    Quincey Morris stabs the Count in the chest. The Count turns to dust.

18. What becomes of the members of the group after their terrible ordeal?
    Mina is completely healed, and she and Jonathan have a happy life
    together. They have a son whom they name Quincey after their
    Texan friend. Quincey Morris had been stabbed by one of the
    men driving the cart carrying the box, and he dies from his wound.
    Lord Goldaming is happily married as is Dr. Seward. Van Helsing
    visits the Harkers.

STUDY GUIDE/QUIZ QUESTIONS - *Dracula*
Multiple Choice Format

Chapters 1 and 2:

1. What is the setting of the first part of the story?
    a. London, England
    b. Carpathian Mountains
    c. America
    d. Mount Everest

2. What does Jonathan Harker find waiting for him when he arrives at the Golden Krone Hotel?
    a. His fiancée, Mina had arrived to surprise him.
    b. There is a letter from Count Dracula.
    c. There is a coach waiting to take him to his final destination.
    d. There is a letter from his fiancée Mina.

3. Why does the hotel landlady beg Jonathan not to continue his journey?
    a. It is the Eve of St. George's Day, and at midnight all evil things will have full sway.
    b. It is a full moon and at midnight all evil things will have full sway.
    c. She begs him to wait until the weather is better.
    d. She begs him to stay with her to protect her from the Count.

4. What does the landlady of the hotel give Jonathan for protection against evil?
    a. She gives him a Bible.
    b. She gives him a crucifix.
    c. She gives him a bag of herbs.
    d. She gives him a kiss.

5. What does **not** fit the description of the driver who meets Jonathan at the Borgo Pass?
    a. He is a short man.
    b. He has a long brown beard.
    c. He is wearing a great black hat.
    d. His eyes seemed red in the lamplight.

6. What does Jonathan find strange about his carriage ride to Castle Dracula?
    a. It is cold outside, but Jonathan stays warm in the carriage.
    b. Jonathan feels they are traveling over and over the same ground.
    c. The carriage driver will not talk to Jonathan.
    d. Jonathan keeps falling asleep.

Dracula Multiple Choice Questions Chapters 1-2 page 2

7. During Jonathan Harker's ride to Castle Dracula, what is "all so strange and uncanny that a dreadful fear came upon [him]"?
    a. The wind suddenly stops and everything becomes instantly calm.
    b. The Count suddenly appears in the middle of the road.
    c. The caleche driver seems to command the wolves to stop howling, and they do.
    d. A wheel breaks suddenly, forcing them to stop in the dark forest.

8. What is it about the caleche driver that seems to make the biggest impression on Jonathan Harker?
    a. Jonathan cannot help but marvel at the control he has over the wolves.
    b. Jonathan cannot help but marvel at the man's great strength.
    c. Jonathan cannot help but marvel at the man's great size.
    d. Jonathan cannot help but marvel at the man's command of the horses.

9. Describe the man who greets Jonathan Harker at Castle Dracula.
    a. He is a tall old man.
    b. He is clean shaven save for a long white moustache.
    c. He is dressed all in black.
    d. All of the above

10. Who are the "children of the night?"
    a. the homeless children wandering the streets
    b. the bats that fly in large winding circles above the trees
    c. the howling wolves
    d. the souls of the recently departed

11. What does Jonathan Harker notice is absent from every room he enters in the castle?
    a. books
    b. mirrors
    c. candles
    d. pictures

12. What does the Count want Jonathan Harker to teach him while at Castle Dracula?
    a. He wants to learn how to purchase real estate.
    b. He wants to speak perfect English.
    c. He wants to learn how to shoot a rifle.
    d. He wants to speak perfect French.

Dracula Multiple Choice Questions Chapters 1-2 page 3

13. What is Jonathan Harker's occupation, and what is his purpose for coming to Transylvania?
    a. He is a college professor who has come to teach the Count English.
    b. He is an attorney who has come to make an offer to buy Castle Dracula.
    c. He is an attorney who has come to close a real estate transaction for a house the Count has purchased in England.
    d. He is a doctor who has come to find the reason for Renfield's madness.

14. When Jonathan Harker looks in his shaving mirror, what peculiar thing does he notice about the Count?
    a. The Count has no reflection in the mirror.
    b. The Count has not changed clothes since the night before.
    c. The Count seems paler than he was on the previous evening.
    d. The Count appears to have grown younger.

15. What surprises Jonathan Harker when he tries to explore the outdoor grounds of Castle Dracula?
    a. The doors leading out of the castle are all locked.
    b. There is a large den of wolves living in a nearby cave.
    c. His window faces a large precipice that juts out over the sea.
    d. Castle Dracula is the only building for miles around.

Chapters 3 and 4:

1. What are Jonathan Harker's thoughts after he discovers the Count laying the table in the dining room?
   a. He thinks the Count has found his secret journal.
   b. He realizes he and the Count are alone in the castle.
   c. He thinks about a secret passage he found leading from his room to the Count's room.
   d. He realizes that he has misjudged the thoughtful Count.

2. Count Dracula claims to be the ancestor of what famous warrior?
   a. He claims to be descended from Genghis Kon.
   b. He claims to be descended from King Author.
   c. He claims to be descended from Attila the Hun.
   d. He claims to be descended from the devil himself.

3. What does the Count warn Jonathan not to do when he is alone at night?
   a. He tells Jonathan not to wander outdoors.
   b. He tells Jonathan not to fall asleep with a candle burning.
   c. He tells Jonathan not to fall asleep in any room other than his own.
   d. He tells Jonathan not to trust anyone who comes to the castle.

4. Describe the way Jonathan Harker sees the Count leave the castle.
   a. He sees the Count turn into a wolf and jump over the wall.
   b. He sees the Count turn into a bat and fly away.
   c. He sees the Count leave in a carriage.
   d. He sees the Count scale down the wall, like a lizard.

5. Jonathan Harker falls asleep in the parlor. What does he see upon waking?
   a. A large wolf has gotten into the castle and is staring hungrily at Jonathan.
   b. He sees three beautiful women who try to seduce him.
   c. He sees the Count coming out from a secret chamber hidden behind the wall.
   d. He sees the lights flicker strangely as a storm brews outside.

6. What is the Count's reaction to finding the women with Jonathan Harker?
   a. He is happy Jonathan has had company.
   b. He is angry, and he flings them violently aside.
   c. He is surprised and leaves them alone with Jonathan.
   d. He is angry, but he understands the women want company.

7. What does Jonathan Harker believe he hears coming from the bag the Count had thrown to the floor?
   a. a half-smothered child
   b. a cat
   c. a bat
   d. a rat

Dracula Multiple Choice Questions Chapters 3-4 page 2

8. What happens to the women and the bag?
    a. They seemed to fade into the rays of moonlight and disappear.
    b. The women disappear, and the Count keeps the bag.
    c. Jonathan grabs the bag, and the women chase him.
    d. The women carry the bag out to another room.

9. The Count instructs Jonathan to write three letters home. What is the content of these letters?
    a. His work in Transylvania is nearly done, and he will be leaving soon.
    b. He would be leaving the castle the next morning.
    c. He had left the castle and has arrived in Bistritz.
    d. All the above

10. Jonathan attempts to send letters home without the Count reading them. What happens to the letters?
    a. The gypsies throw the letters into the river.
    b. The letters make it to Mina.
    c. The Count intercepts the letters.
    d. Jonathan losses his nerve and never tries to send the letters.

11. What does Jonathan discover upon waking on 31 May?
    a. He sees the Count leaving the castle in his traveling clothes.
    b. All of his personal papers and traveling clothes are gone.
    c. His journal is missing.
    d. The Count has left his door unlocked.

12. What do the Slovaks deliver to the castle?
    a. They deliver the week's food.
    b. They deliver letters for Count Dracula.
    c. They deliver empty large wooden boxes.
    d. The deliver meat for the Count's wolves.

13. When Count Dracula leaves the castle on 24 June, what does Jonathan Harker notice?
    a. The Count is wearing the caleche driver's clothes.
    b. The Count is wearing Slovak-style clothing.
    c. The Count is wearing Jonathan Harker's traveling clothes.
    d. The Count is dressed in a long, flowing, black cape.

14. Jonathan goes to the window when he hears the agonizing cry of a women. What does she yell upon seeing Jonathan's face at the window?
    a. "Run. Get out! He will kill you."
    b. "Monster! Give me back my child!"
    c. "Monster! How can you protect the Count!"
    d. "Help! Help me! The wolves are coming!"

Dracula Multiple Choice Questions Chapters 3-4 page 3

15. What happens to the woman as she continues to bang on the door of the Count's castle at night?
    a. The Count opens the door and slits her throat.
    b. Wolves attack and kill her.
    c. She is attacked by ravenous bats.
    d. Three women surround her and kill her.

16. Jonathan decides to climb the wall of the castle into the Count's room. Which of these things does he **not** find in the Count's rooms?
    a. an old ruined chapel
    b. boxes filled with dirt
    c. the Count
    d. a key

17. Jonathan tells the Count that he wants to leave the night of 29 June, but he suddenly changes his mind. Why?
    a. The three voluptuous women are waiting just outside the door.
    b. There are hungry wolves snarling at the door.
    c. He realizes that it is too late to catch the last evening train.
    d. The Count tells him that he will kill him before he can reach the gate.

18. What does Jonathan Harker find when he goes back to the Count's room to look for a key to the door?
    a. He finds the Count in one of the boxes, and he looks younger.
    b. He finds the key to the Counts door but not to the gate.
    c. He finds nothing in the Count's room.
    d. He finds the women with another bag.

Chapters 5 and 6:

1. What is the relationship between Mina Murray and Jonathan Harker?
   a. They are brother and sister.
   b. They are second cousins.
   c. They are engaged to be married.
   d. They are close friends of Lucy.

2. What kind of institution does Dr. Seward run?
   a. hotel
   b. insane asylum
   c. hospital
   d. sanitarium

3. Who did **not** propose marriage to Lucy?
   a. Jonathan Harker
   b. Arthur Holmwood
   c. Dr. John Seward
   d. Quincy Morris

4. Who is Quincey Morris?
   a. He is Lucy's brother.
   b. He is Arthur Holmwood's friend.
   c. He is Mina's father.
   d. He is Jonathan Harker's employer.

5. Which of the marriage proposals does Lucy accept?
   a. She decides to accept Dr. Seward's marriage proposal.
   b. She decides to accept Jonathan Harker's marriage proposal.
   c. She decides to accept Quincey Morris's marriage proposal.
   d. She decides to accept Arthur Holmwood's marriage proposal.

6. What is the name of the patient who seems to be of most interest to Dr. Seward?
   a. Jonathan Harker
   b. Quincey Morris
   c. Renfield
   d. Mrs. Westenra

7. What does the old man that Mina and Lucy meet claim about the tombstones in the cemetery?
   a. The epitaphs are lies.
   b. They are the oldest tombstones in the county.
   c. They tell the story of those who lived there in the past.
   d. The tombstones are stained with the blood of innocent victims.

Dracula Multiple Choice Questions Chapters 5-6 page 2

8. Which is Renfield's systematic way of collecting lives?
    a. He uses the inductive method.
    b. He catches flies, feeds them to spiders, then feeds the spiders to the birds.
    c. He uses a proactive method.
    d. He kills the spiders and birds, and flies feed on the rotting carcasses.

9. What unusual thing does Renfield eat?
    a. Renfield bites his own arm and drinks his own blood.
    b. Renfield eats his flies, spiders and birds.
    c. Renfield eats only raw food.
    d. Renfield eats the scraps left from the other patients.

10. What odd, recent behavior of Lucy is disturbing to Mina?
    a. Lucy has begun biting her nails.
    b. Lucy continuously talks of her fiancé and does not understand Mina's feelings.
    c. Lucy refuses to speak of her wedding.
    d. Lucy has begun sleep walking.

Chapters 7 and 8:

1. Describe the mysterious schooner's entrance into the harbor.
    a. The schooner sailed into the harbor late at night.
    b. The schooner was blown into the harbor by high winds.
    c. The schooner never made it into the harbor.
    d. The schooner crashed into the rocks at the mouth of the harbor.

2. What is discovered on board the mysterious schooner?
    a. It is completely abandoned.
    b. The dead captain is tied to the ship's wheel.
    c. The first mate had tethered himself to the main mast.
    d. A mysterious man in black ran down the gangplank.

3. What is the name of the schooner, and where does she come from?
    a. Czarina Catherine, Dardanelles
    b. Demeter, Vanra
    c. Borgo, Carpathia
    d. Bristritz, Transylvania

4. What is the only living thing on the ship?
    a. a large dog
    b. a mysterious man in black
    c. a large bat hanging from the main mast
    d. a large grey wolf

5. According to the captain's addendum to the ship's log, what happened to the men on the ship?
    a. The men went insane one by one and jumped off the ship.
    b. The men ate rotten food, got sick and died.
    c. The men went insane and killed one another.
    d. The men began to disappear one by one.

6. What does the captain see on the last night aboard the ship?
    a. The first mate went mad and jumped overboard.
    b. A man in black with glowing red eyes approached him.
    c. A huge black dog came at him.
    d. A giant bat circled overhead.

7. What happens to the old man who befriended Mina and Lucy?
    a. He presides over the captain's funeral.
    b. It is believed that he leapt from the cliff; Mina and Lucy doubt this.
    c. He is found in the cemetery with his neck broken.
    d. He begs Lucy and Mina to leave as soon as possible, and then disappears.

Dracula Multiple Choice Questions Chapters 7-8 page 2

8. On August 11th what does Mina discover when she awakens in the night?
    a. A large bat has entered their room.
    b. Wolves are howling loudly outside their window.
    c. There is a mysterious fog filling the room.
    d. Lucy has disappeared.

9. What does Mina see in the moonlit churchyard when she goes looking for Lucy?
    a. Mina sees a dark, sinister figure bent over Lucy.
    b. Mina sees a large dog.
    c. Mina sees a large bat circling over her head.
    d. Mina sees Lucy ready to fling herself from the cliff.

10. What is Mina most concerned about for Lucy's sake as they walk home from the churchyard?
    a. She is concerned that Arthur will be upset and refuse to marry Lucy.
    b. She is concerned she will cut her feet and fall off the path.
    c. She is concerned about Lucy's reputation and that she will get sick.
    d. She is concerned Lucy will wake up and be frightened.

11. What makes Mina think that she pricked Lucy accidentally with a safety pin?
    a. She notices blood on Lucy's pillow case.
    b. Lucy complains of an unexplained wound on her arm.
    c. Mina notices two small marks on Lucy's neck.
    d. Lucy has wrapped a bandage around a wound.

12. On the night of August 13th what does Mina see outside the window?
    a. a wolf
    b. a bat
    c. a thick mist
    d. a strange man

13. On August 14th Mina and Lucy notice a dark figure seated alone in the cemetery just before sundown. What was it that startles Mina about his appearance?
    a. his eyes which seemed to look like burning flames
    b. his black clothing
    c. his uncanny resemblance to Jonathan
    d. his smile

14. On August 18th what change does Mina begin to notice in Lucy?
    a. Lucy has stopped sleep walking.
    b. Lucy is growing more and more tired everyday.
    c. Lucy seems better in spite of looking sadly pale and wan.
    d. Lucy has regained her coloring and is very cheerful.

Dracula Multiple Choice Questions Chapters 7-8 page 3

15. What news does Mina receive that makes her both joyful and anxious at the same time?
    a. She finally hears word of her fiancé, Jonathan Harker, but he is very ill.
    b. She learns that Lucy will marry Arthur; she thinks that he is not good for Lucy.
    c. She learns that Jonathan has been made a partner in his firm; she worries about him working long hours.
    d. She has been offered a secretarial position, but she is not sure she wants it.

16. What changes are taking place in Renfield?
    a. He has become excited and is sniffing around in his cell like a dog.
    b. He is growing weaker and weaker by the day.
    c. He is eating more flies and not bathing.
    d. He has become very relaxed and is talking with Dr. Seward.

17. What does not happen when Renfield escapes from the asylum?
    a. He is caught without a fight.
    b. Someone or something wrenches the cell window from the wall.
    c. He goes to the Carfax estate.
    d. He climbs out the hole in the wall.

Chapters 9 and 10:

1. How does Mina describe Jonathan in her letter to Lucy?
    a. Mina tells Lucy he is back to his old self.
    b. Mina tells Lucy he is thin, pale, and weak-looking.
    c. Mina tells Lucy he very sick and can not get out of bed.
    d. Mina tells Lucy he is very banged-up, but he will be fine.

2. What request does Jonathan make of Mina regarding his notebook?
    a. He wants her to read it so that she will understand what he's been through.
    b. He wants her to burn it.
    c. He wants her to keep it in a safe place and read it only if she wants to.
    d. He wants her to pass it on to Dr. Seward to help with Lucy's condition.

3. Where were Mina and Jonathan married?
    a. Mina and Jonathan were married at the insane asylum.
    b. Mina and Jonathan were married at Hillingham.
    c. Mina and Jonathan were married at the hospital.
    d. Mina and Jonathan were married in Transylvania.

4. What does Mina do with Jonathan's notebook?
    a. She reads it and is horrified.
    b. She burns it.
    c. She wraps it and ties it with ribbon as a wedding gift to Jonathan.
    d. She gives it to Dr. Seward.

5. What daily pattern has developed in Renfield since Dr. Seward confined him to a straight jacket and a padded room?
    a. He sits in the corner of the room all day.
    b. He is wild and crazy all day.
    c. He is violent during the day and quiet from moonrise to sunrise.
    d. He refuses to eat.

6. How does Renfield escape a second time?
    a. He breaks out through the window.
    b. He pretends to be sick so the attendant will open the door to his cell.
    c. He hides behind the door and runs out when the attendant comes in to look for him.
    d. When the attendant opens the cell he knocks him down and runs.

7. What begins happening to Lucy upon her return home to Hillingham?
    a. She begins sleepwalking.
    b. She has terrible nightmares.
    c. She begins to feel very depressed.
    d. She is getting very thin.

Dracula Multiple Choice Questions Chapters 9-10 page 2

8. Arthur Holmwood asks Dr. Seward to examine Lucy. What are Dr. Seward's findings regarding Lucy?
    a. He thinks that she has a rare blood disease.
    b. He finds that her muscles are beginning to deteriorate.
    c. He finds nothing at all to be concerned about.
    d. He can not find any functional disturbance, but is concerned about her weakness and appearance.

9. What is Lucy's condition when Dr. Seward and Van Helsing visit her on September 7th?
    a. Lucy is sitting up in bed and eating soup.
    b. Lucy is in a coma.
    c. Lucy is ghastly, chalkily pale and having trouble breathing.
    d. Lucy is in a trance-like state.

10. What action does Van Helsing believe is necessary to keep Lucy alive?
    a. chemotherapy
    b. a tight tourniquet around the wound on her throat to keep it from bleeding
    c. angioplasty
    d. a blood transfusion

11. Who arrives and offers to help in Van Helsing's first treatment of Lucy?
    a. Dr. Seward
    b. Arthur Holmwood
    c. Quincey Morris
    d. Jonathan Harker

12. What specific instructions does Van Helsing give Dr. Seward regarding Lucy before he leaves for Amsterdam?
    a. to make sure she gets up and walks every hour to increase circulation
    b. to be sure she eats at least five small meals a day
    c. to never leave her unattended for any reason
    d. to make sure she drinks at least sixty-four ounces of water daily

13. What does Van Helsing discover upon his return to Hillingham?
    a. Lucy's mother has died.
    b. Lucy is feeling like her old self again.
    c. Mina has come down with the same illness as Lucy.
    d. Dr. Seward left Lucy alone, and she is very ill.

14. Who aids Van Helsing in the second transfusion to Lucy?
    a. Quincey Morris
    b. Jonathan Harker
    c. Abraham Van Helsing
    d. Dr. Seward

Dracula Multiple Choice Questions Chapters 9-10 page 3

15. What is in the package that Van Helsing receives from abroad?
    a. garlic flowers
    b. tulips
    c. pieces of the Host (consecrated communion wafers)
    d. a medical journal to help him in his treatment of Lucy

Chapters 11 and 12:

1. What does Mrs. Westenra tell Van Helsing that causes him to break down in tears?
    a. Lucy is dead.
    b. Mina is severely ill just as Lucy is.
    c. She threw away the flowers in Lucy's bedroom and opened the windows.
    d. Dr. Seward has given up and left.

2. Who volunteers his arm for Lucy's third blood transfusion?
    a. Quincey Morris
    b. Jonathan Harker
    c. Abraham Van Helsing
    d. a child

3. What happens as soon as the zookeeper finished telling his tale to the reporter?
    a. All of the animals in the zoo begin to howl.
    b. A police man comes to tell the zookeeper the wolf has been killed.
    c. The wolf comes back to the zoo peacefully, on his own.
    d. The wolf crashes through the zookeeper's window and kills the reporter.

4. After he is attached by Renfield, what act does Dr. Seward witness that "positively sickened" him?
    a. Three women mysteriously appear and try to seduce him.
    b. A large grey wolf tears a man's throat out.
    c. Renfield laps blood off the floor like a dog.
    d. Dracula attacks Lucy.

5. What happens to Lucy's mother?
    a. She dies of a heart attack when a wolf jumps through Lucy's window.
    b. She left the country because her health was failing so badly.
    c. She is hospitalized after collapsing in Lucy's room.
    d. She falls down the stairs when she is trying to get help for Lucy.

6. What do Dr. Seward and Van Helsing see when they enter Lucy's room?
    a. Mrs. Westenra is dead, and Lucy is near death.
    b. They see a grey wolf biting at Lucy's throat.
    c. Lucy is at the window getting ready to jump.
    d. Lucy is dead, and Mrs. Westenra is near death.

7. Who gives blood in Lucy's fourth transfusion?
    a. Quincey Morris
    b. Jonathan Harker
    c. Abraham Van Helsing
    d. a child

Dracula Multiple Choice Questions Chapters 11-12 page 2

8. What strange action does Lucy do just as she is falling asleep after the fourth transfusion?
    a. Lucy gets out of bed, goes to the window and comes back to bed.
    b. Lucy pantomimes tearing the note Van Helsing takes from her.
    c. Lucy pantomimes stringing garlic flowers.
    d. Lucy dumps the garlic flowers on the floor.

9. What is Renfield's reaction when some men remove several heavy boxes from Carfax?
    a. He attacks them.
    b. He attempts to help them move the boxes.
    c. He wants to know where the boxes were being taken.
    d. He suddenly becomes very frightened.

10. What alarming changes occur in Lucy's physical condition?
    a. Lucy's finger nails have grown twice as long over night.
    b. Lucy's teeth have become longer and sharper.
    c. Lucy's hair has started falling out.
    d. Lucy is now blind.

11. What does Van Helsing do when Arthur attempts to kiss Lucy?
    a. Van Helsing leaves the room to give them privacy.
    b. Van Helsing pulls Arthur away violently and throws him across the room.
    c. Van Helsing tells Arthur he must only kiss Lucy's hand.
    d. Van Helsing tells Arthur it is not safe to kiss Lucy.

12. What does Lucy ask Van Helsing when she awakens from her trance-like stupor?
    a. She asks him to guard Arthur and give her peace.
    b. She asks him to never tell Arthur the truth about the blood transfusions.
    c. She asks him to take her to the window so she can see the sun one last time.
    d. She asks him to watch over Mina.

13. What ultimately becomes of Lucy Westenra?
    a. Dr. Van Helsing is able to find a cure for her.
    b. She marries Arthur Holmwood.
    c. She dies.
    d. She breaks her engagement to Arthur Holmwood and marries Quincey Morris.

Chapters 13 and 14:

1. What do Dr. Seward and Van Helsing notice about Lucy's body when they go to pay their respects?
   a. Lucy looks like her old self.
   b. Lucy looks very thin and her teeth were visible.
   c. Lucy is more beautiful in death and seems very life-like.
   d. Lucy is smiling, which frightens them.

2. What does Van Helsing want to do with Lucy's body?
   a. He wants to burn it.
   b. He wants to bury it in consecrated soil as soon as possible.
   c. He wants to cut off her head and take out her heart.
   d. He wants to douse it with holy water and place the Host in her mouth.

3. What happens when the maid sits by Lucy's body during the night?
   a. Lucy attacks her; she is not really dead.
   b. The maid steals the crucifix off of Lucy's body.
   c. The maid hears wings brushing at the window and sees a large bat outside.
   d. The maid falls asleep and is awakened by a mysterious man in black.

4. Who is Lord Godalming?
   a. It is Quincey Morris's real title.
   b. He is a lawyer who wants to settle the Westenra estate.
   c. Lord Godalming is Arthur Holmwood's title after the death of his father.
   d. He is a patient of Dr. Seward.

5. What request does Van Helsing make of Arthur regarding the Westenra estate?
   a. Van Helsing asks Arthur to let Jonathan Harker settle the estate.
   b. Van Helsing asks Arthur to see Lucy's letters and diary.
   c. Van Helsing asks Arthur to leave the house to Mina.
   d. Van Helsing asks Arthur to leave the house to Dr. Seward.

6. What does Jonathan Harker see that causes him to go pale as he walks down Piccadilly?
   a. He sees Count Dracula, and he is younger.
   b. He sees Lucy with a child.
   c. He sees Mina with another man.
   d. He sees a wolf tear a man's throat out.

7. After Jonathan Harker's sudden relapse, what does Mina declare it is time for her to do?
   a. She will read Jonathan's journal.
   b. She will call for a doctor to help him.
   c. She decides to have him committed at Dr. Seward's asylum.
   d. She decides to give herself to the Count to save Jonathan.

Dracula Multiple Choice Questions Chapters 13-14 page 2

8. What secret do Dr. Seward, Van Helsing, and Quincy Morris vow to keep from Arthur?
    a. They vow never to tell Arthur about the other marriage proposals.
    b. They vow never to tell Arthur Lucy is a vampire.
    c. They vow never to tell Arthur about the other blood transfusions.
    d. They vow never to tell Arthur Lucy secretly loved Quincey.

9. What strange occurrences begin taking place in Hampstead not long after Lucy's funeral?
    a. Children have begun to disappear.
    b. Dogs and cats have begun to disappear.
    c. Rats have begun to disappear.
    d. Bats and wolves seem to be gathering in the area.

10. What does Mina learn that upsets her terribly?
    a. She learns of Lucy's death.
    b. She reads Jonathan's diary and knows the terrible ordeal he went through.
    c. She learns the Count will be stronger after Lucy's death.
    d. She reads Dr. Seward's journal and knows how Lucy has suffered.

11. What does Mina plan to do with Jonathan's diary?
    a. Mina plans to burn Jonathan's diary.
    b. Mina plans to type Jonathan's diary so the others can read it.
    c. Mina plans to wrap Jonathan's diary back up and never tell Jonathan she has read it.
    d. Mina plans to show the diary to Dr. Seward.

12. After reading Mina's letter to Lucy, Dr. Van Helsing requests a visit with Mina. What specific event does he ask Mina to share in detail?
    a. Mina is asked to give an account of the night she found Lucy in the graveyard.
    b. Mina is asked to reveal Lucy's true feelings about her marriage decision.
    c. Mina is asked to describe her last visit with Lucy.
    d. Mina is asked to describe their walks together in Whitby.

13. What does Mina allow Van Helsing to read?
    a. Mina allows Van Helsing to read the letters Lucy had sent to her.
    b. Mina allows Van Helsing to read both her and Jonathan's diaries.
    c. Mina allows Van Helsing to read Jonathan's diary.
    d. Mina allows Van Helsing to read her diary.

14. What change comes over Jonathan after reading Van Helsing's note about the diaries?
    a. He is angry Mina has allowed anyone to read his diary.
    b. He becomes stronger and more self-assured.
    c. He becomes very depressed and will not speak to Van Helsing.
    d. He is happy the truth is finally out.

Dracula Multiple Choice Questions Chapters 13-14 page 3

15. Van Helsing is trying to make Dr. Seward accept and understand Lucy's death and what is happening to the children of Hampstead. Which of the following is not one of the unexplained mysteries of the natural world that Van Helsing uses in his explanation?
    a. There are bats that exist that drain the blood of cattle and horses.
    b. There are such tortured souls that live as vampires throughout centuries.
    c. Tortoises, elephants and parrots live longer than generations of men.
    d. The Indian fakir can rise from the dead after several years.

16. How does Van Helsing explain the bite marks found on the children of Hampstead Heath?
    a. He claims that a bat made them
    b. He claims that Lucy made them.
    c. He claims that a wolf made them.
    d. He claims that a large dog made them.

Chapters 15, 16, and 17:

1. Where is the first place Dr. Seward and Van Helsing go in an attempt to prove Van Helsing's theories about Lucy are true.
    a. They go to Transylvania.
    b. They go to Carfax.
    c. The go to the hospital in Hampstead.
    d. They go to the church.

2. What does Dr. Vincent believe made the marks on the children's throats?
    a. He claims that a bat made them.
    b. He claims that Lucy made them.
    c. He claims that a wolf made them.
    d. He claims that a large dog made them.

3. What do Van Helsing and Dr. Seward find when they open Lucy's coffin?
    a. Lucy looks more beautiful than ever.
    b. It is empty.
    c. Her body is beginning to deteriorate.
    d. It is filled with dirt.

4. What do Van Helsing and Dr. Seward do after exiting Lucy's tomb?
    a. They go to town and have dinner.
    b. They hide in the cemetery to watch for any activity.
    c. They return to the asylum to talk to Renfield.
    d. They go to the Westenra estate to find Lucy.

5. What do Van Helsing and Dr. Seward do with the child they find in the cemetery?
    a. They take the child to the hospital.
    b. They take the child to the police.
    c. They leave the child where the police could easily find it.
    d. They take the child to the asylum for examination.

6. What do Dr. Seward and Van Helsing discover when they return to Lucy's tomb the following afternoon?
    a. Someone has stolen Lucy's body.
    b. Her body looks more beautiful than ever.
    c. Someone has nailed the coffin shut and sealed it with wax.
    d. The tomb is destroyed.

7. Why does Van Helsing hesitate to immediately do what needs to be done to Lucy's body in order to bring her soul peace?
    a. He is afraid he will not be able to do what needs to be done.
    b. It is too close to sunset.
    c. He believes Arthur must know the truth about Lucy's death.
    d. Dr. Seward stops him.

Dracula Multiple Choice Questions Chapters 15-17 page 2

8. How does Van Helsing intend to keep Lucy inside her tomb at night?
    a. Van Helsing places a guard at the tomb.
    b. Van Helsing places garlic and a crucifix in the tomb.
    c. Van Helsing hires a Priest to bless Lucy's body.
    d. Van Helsing places the Host on Lucy's body.

9. What news does Van Helsing share with Arthur and Quincey Morris?
    a. Van Helsing tells them Mina has become ill like Lucy.
    b. Van Helsing tells them Jonathan has found the Count's boxes.
    c. Van Helsing tells them Dr. Seward has killed the Count.
    d. Van Helsing tells them Lucy is one of the Un-Dead.

10. What does Arthur unwillingly agree to do?
    a. Arthur agrees to share the Westenra estate with Van Helsing.
    b. Arthur agrees to cutting off Lucy's head and putting a steak through her heart.
    c. Arthur agrees to visit Lucy's tomb with Van Helsing.
    d. Arthur agrees to let Van Helsing do as he sees fit with Lucy.

11. Dr. Seward, Van Helsing, Quincey Morris, and Arthur find Lucy's tomb empty. What do they see in the cemetery the same night?
    a. They see Lucy in vampire form and witness her attack of a child.
    b. They see the Count enter Lucy's tomb.
    c. They see a child follow Lucy to her tomb.
    d. They see the Count carry Lucy's body away.

12. What is Arthur's reaction when Lucy speaks to him in the cemetery?
    a. Arthur is overcome with grief and falls to the ground.
    b. Arthur is happy to see Lucy and runs to her.
    c. Arthur is mesmerized; he goes to Lucy as if in a trance.
    d. Arthur is frightened and runs from the cemetery.

13. How does Van Helsing protect Arthur from Lucy's temptation?
    a. Van Helsing grabs Arthur and holds him until Quincey kills Lucy.
    b. Van Helsing jumps between them and holds up a crucifix towards Lucy.
    c. Van Helsing kills Lucy before she can get to Arthur.
    d. Van Helsing drives Lucy's back to her coffin with the Host.

14. According to Van Helsing, what do the Eastern Europeans call the Un-Dead?
    a. nosferatu
    b. vampire
    c. she-devil
    d. satan

Dracula Multiple Choice Questions Chapters 15-17 page 3

15. Who strikes the blow that sets Lucy's soul free?
    a. Van Helsing
    b. Quincey Morris
    c. Dr. Seward
    d. Arthur Holmwood

16. What happens to Lucy after the stake is driven through her heart?
    a. She is no longer a vile creature, she is the sweet Lucy the men had known.
    b. She catches on fire.
    c. She turns to dust and blows away in the wind.
    d. She looks at Arthur and smiles.

17. When the men exit Lucy's tomb for the last time, what does each strongly swear to do?
    a. Each swears to believe in God.
    b. Each swears to find Count Dracula and destroy him.
    c. Each swears they will never speak of Lucy again.
    d. Each swears to keep the events of the evening a secret.

18. Who or what does Van Helsing find waiting for him when he returns to the hotel?
    a. Mina
    b. a telegram from Mina saying she is on her way to meet with Van Helsing
    c. the police waiting to talk with him
    d. the Count waiting in his room

19. What does Van Helsing give to Dr. Seward before he leaves for Amsterdam?
    a. He gives him a crucifix to protect him.
    b. He gives him the transfusion equipment in the event Dr. Seward needs to give Mina a transfusion.
    c. He gives him Lucy's journal to read.
    d. He gives him the Harkers' journals to read.

20. Who does Dr. Seward encourage to stay at his home?
    a. Mina Harker
    b. Quincey Morris
    c. Van Helsing
    d. Arthur Holmwood

21. Dr. Seward keeps his own personal diary on phonograph. What does Mina intend to do with Dr. Seward's wax cylinders?
    a. Mina is going to listen to each cylinder to check for clues about Dracula.
    b. Mina is going to transcribe his diary with her typewriter.
    c. Mina is going to burn the cylinders to protect Lucy.
    d. Mina is going to transcribe his diary in short hand.

Dracula Multiple Choice Questions Chapters 15-17 page 4

22. What is ironic about the discovery of the Count's possible hiding place?
    a. It is next door to Dr. Seward's asylum.
    b. It is in the basement of the Westenra estate.
    c. It is in the attic of Dr. Seward's asylum.
    d. It is in the middle of London's business district where there are many people.

23. Who does Dr. Seward realize may be strangely linked to Count Dracula?
    a. Mina
    b. Renfield
    c. Lucy
    d. Van Helsing

24. In Whitby, Jonathan tracks down the location of the Count's fifty large boxes. Where are they located?
    a. The fifty boxes have been delivered to fifty different address.
    b. The fifty boxes have been delivered to the Westenra estate.
    c. The fifty boxes have been delivered to Carfax.
    d. The fifty boxes are sitting at the Varna port.

25. What happens that causes Arthur to swear that he would be a life-long brother to Mina Harker?
    a. Mina comforts him over the death of Lucy.
    b. He promises Lucy he would always be a brother to Mina.
    c. Mina is all alone, and she asks him to always look after her.
    d. He is in love with Mina, but she belongs to Jonathan.

Chapters 18 and 19:

1. Mina asks Dr. Seward if she can see Renfield. What is Renfield's method of "tidying up" his cell before her visit?
    a. Renfield folds the blanket on his cot and sweeps the floor.
    b. Renfield eats all of the flies and spiders he has captured.
    c. Renfield licks the floor like a dog.
    d. Renfield cleans the floor with his drinking water.

2. What is Rienfield's explanation for eating live flies and spiders?
    a. He claims they give him the protein he needs to stay healthy.
    b. He claims they taste better alive then dead.
    c. He claims their blood will give him an indefinitely prolonged life.
    d. He only eats them because there is never enough food.

3. Which of the following is not one of the powers that Van Helsing claims Count Dracula has as a nosferatu?
    a. He can be a shape-shifter (into a mist or an animal).
    b. He has power over weather.
    c. He has eternal life.
    d. He can read anyone's mind.

4. What does Van Helsing claim is the greatest danger that the men face as they attempt to destroy Dracula?
    a. They could all become vampires.
    b. They could be arrested for murder.
    c. They could all die.
    d. They might never be able to go back to London.

5. Which of the following is not one of a vampire's limitations according to Van Helsing?
    a. He can eat no food except blood.
    b. He casts no shadow or reflection.
    c. He cannot leave his box in the daytime.
    d. He cannot enter a place unless invited to do so.

6. What does Quincey Morris claim he was shooting at when he broke the parlor window at Dr. Seward's home?
    a. a wolf
    b. a bat
    c. the Count
    d. a rat

Dracula Multiple Choice Questions Chapters 18-19 page 2

7. What does Van Helsing tell Mina about the quest to hunt down the Count?
    a. He tells Mina it will be over soon.
    b. He tells Mina it will be harder than she could ever imagine.
    c. He tells Mina she can no longer be involved because it is too dangerous.
    d. He tells Mina the Count has a head start; he will be difficult to catch.

8. What is Renfield's reaction when Dr. Seward tells him that he may not leave the asylum?
    a. He becomes violent and attacks the doctor.
    b. He becomes sarcastic and tells the doctor that the Master would take care of him.
    c. He becomes sullen and quiet and refuses to speak to anyone.
    d. He becomes hysterical and begs to be allowed to leave under any condition.

9. How does Van Helsing prepare Dr. Seward and the others to go to Carfax to find the Count?
    a. Van Helsing reads a prayer from the Bible.
    b. Van Helsing gets a Priest to bless each of the men.
    c. Van Helsing gives each a Winchester rifle.
    d. Van Helsing gives each man a crucifix, a gun, a knife, and the Host.

10. What do Dr. Seward and the others notice the most as they enter the old chapel at Carfax?
    a. The chapel is filled with old tombs.
    b. The chapel reeks of a putrid smell.
    c. Count Dracula is asleep in one of the coffins.
    d. The floor is littered with dead bodies.

11. When thousands of rats swarm the chapel, how are the men able to continue searching?
    a. Quincey locks the rats in one room.
    b. Quincey shoots his Winchester rifle, and it frightens the rats away.
    c. Arthur calls a pack of dogs with a whistle and they attack the rats.
    d. Arthur drops a oil lamp on the floor, and the flames frighten the rats away.

12. How many boxes were missing from Carfax of the original fifty boxes shipped from Transylvania to London?
    a. 29
    b. 9
    c. 6
    d. 21

13. What does Jonathan Harker notice about his wife when he returns from Carfax?
    a. He notices how peaceful she looks when she is sleeping.
    b. He notices how deeply she is sleeping.
    c. He notices how deathly pale she is.
    d. Answers B & C

Dracula Multiple Choice Questions Chapters 18-19 page 3

14. Describe Van Helsing's meeting with Renfield the morning after the visit to Carfax.
    a. Renfield begs Van Helsing to let him go.
    b. Renfield calls Van Helsing an "old fool."
    c. Renfield attacks Van Helsing and bites him.
    d. Renfield refuses to look a Van Helsing.

15. What is distressing Mina regarding her husband's visit to the Count's house?
    a. The men refuse to tell her any details in order to protect her.
    b. She knows that the Count is aware of their every move.
    c. She believes that her husband has already been bitten by the Count.
    d. She believes that Van Helsing is needlessly leading Jonathan into danger.

16. Why does Mina wish she'd never gone to Whitby to visit Lucy?
    a. Jonathan would have married her sooner.
    b. Lucy would never have started sleepwalking.
    c. Lucy would have come to visit Mina and never been around the Count.
    d. Mina would never have known the Count.

17. What strange dream does Mina describe?
    a. She is flying like a bat over London.
    b. She is laying in a coffin with Lucy.
    c. She sees the Count's face in the clouds.
    d. She sees gleaming red eyes through a mist.

Chapters 20 and 21:

1. Where are the 21 boxes missing from Carfax taken?
    a. six to Piccadilly, six to Mile End, six to Jamaica Lane
    b. six to Piccadilly, six to Jamaica Lane, nine to Mile End
    c. six to Jamaica Lane, six to Mile End, nine to Piccadilly
    d. six to Jamaica Lane, six to Piccadilly, nine to Mile End

2. What change does Jonathan Harker notice about Mina?
    a. Mina is pale, tired, and shudders at the mention of Dracula.
    b. Mina has gotten her color back and is eating.
    c. Mina is avoiding Jonathan and the others.
    d. Mina is sick.

3. Renfield says that he wants life from other beings, but he does not want something else. What is it he does **not** want?
    a. their souls
    b. to have vengeance taken against him
    c. to have to give these lives to the Master
    d. to share life with anyone else

4. Dr. Seward notices that twice Renfield stops himself before uttering a specific word. What word is it?
    a. die
    b. eat
    c. pray
    d. drink

5. After Dr. Seward leaves Renfield, what does the doctor realize?
    a. Renfield is only pretending to be insane.
    b. Renfield is actually terrified of the doctor.
    c. The Count has been in contact with Renfield.
    d. Renfield is in love with Mina Harker.

6. Who do the realtors at Mitchell, Sons, and Candy claim purchased the house in Piccadilly?
    a. Count Dracula
    b. Mina
    c. Lord Godalming
    d. Count de Ville

7. What does Dr. Seward hear that alarms him coming from Renfield's room?
    a. Dr. Seward hears a blood-curdling scream.
    b. Dr. Seward hears Renfield calling to Count Dracula.
    c. Dr. Seward hears a explosion.
    d. Dr. Seward hears Mina's voice.

Dracula Multiple Choice Questions Chapters 20-21 page 2

8. The asylum attendant reports to Dr. Seward that Renfield has met with an accident. What happens to Renfield?
    a. He escapes from the asylum again.
    b. He kills himself because he could not leave the asylum.
    c. An attendant finds him bleeding and broken on his cell floor.
    d. He is shot when he tries to attack an attendant.

9. What procedure does Van Helsing perform on Renfield?
    a. a lobotomy
    b. a procedure to relieve pressure on the brain
    c. an autopsy
    d. an exorcism

10. What does Count Dracula promise Renfield in exchange for letting him into the asylum?
    a. the lives of rats
    b. Mina Harker as his own
    c. the vampire Lucy as a life partner
    d. to share power in their conquest of London

11. Why does Renfield become angry with the Count?
    a. Renfield wants total control of London, not shared control with the Count.
    b. Renfield knows that he cannot have Lucy because she has been destroyed.
    c. The Count promised to release him from the asylum but didn't.
    d. He realized the Count has lied and used him to get to Mina Harker.

12. What does Renfield notice about Mina Harker?
    a. He notices that she is angrier than usual due to the stress of the situation.
    b. He notices that she seems paler and realizes that the Count took her blood.
    c. He notices that her teeth are becoming more pronounced and sharp.
    d. He notices that she stays awake at night and sleeps during the day.

13. What happens between Renfield and Dracula when the Count returns to the asylum?
    a. Renfield begs for forgiveness and the Count lets him out.
    b. The Count feeds on Renfield.
    c. Renfield attacks the Count, and the Count smashes Renfield's face and breaks his back.
    d. Dracula asks Renfield to let him in, and Renfield complies.

14. What do Van Helsing, Dr. Seward, Lord Godalming, and Quincy Morris witness after breaking down the door to the Harker's bedroom?
    a. the Count making Mina drink his blood while Jonathan is asleep
    b. the Count making Jonathan drink blood from Mina's neck
    c. an empty room with an open window
    d. Mina and Jonathan in bed covered in rats

Dracula Multiple Choice Questions Chapters 20-21 page 3

15. Upon escaping, what does the Count do with the typed manuscript and phonograph diary entries?
    a. The Count takes the manuscript and burns the phonograph cylinders.
    b. The Count throws them into the fire.
    c. The Count takes them with him to read.
    d. The Count throws them around the room.

16. Recount Mina's description of her encounter with Dracula.
    a. She holds up a crucifix, and the Count turns to mist.
    b. She is forced to drink Jonathan's blood while he sleeps.
    c. She is forced to drink the Count's blood, or he will kill Jonathan.
    d. The Count drinks her blood, and then she passes out.

Chapters 22 and 23:

1. What do the men discover when they return to Renfield's room?
    a. Renfield is talking to the Count through the window.
    b. Dracula is drinking from Renfields neck.
    c. Renfield is dead.
    d. Renfield is begging the attendant to kill him.

2. What decision do Dr. Seward and Van Helsing make regarding Mina's knowledge of their activities?
    a. They decide to keep Mina in the dark about their plans.
    b. They decide it is best to take Mina into full confidence.
    c. They decide to lie to Mina.
    d. They decide to use Mina to give the Count false information.

3. Mina vows to kill herself if she will endanger the others in any way. Why does Dr. Van Helsing tell her this can not be?
    a. If she kills herself, her soul will be damned forever.
    b. If she kills herself, he would never forgive himself for letting her down.
    c. If she dies before the Count, she will become like him.
    d. If she dies before the Count, she won't be able to help them find him.

4. How does Van Helsing propose to enter the Count's locked house in Piccadilly by daylight without drawing unnecessary attention?
    a. He will pretend to be a contractor who is renovating the house.
    b. Arthur will create a diversion and Van Helsing will break in the back door.
    c. Arthur and Quincey will pretend to be the owners and hire a locksmith.
    d. He will call the real estate company and tell them he is a relative of the owner.

5. Why does Van Helsing say that the group will be unlikely to run into the Count during day?
    a. He knows that the Count is bound to his box in Carfax with a piece of the Host.
    b. Vampires cannot come out of their coffins during the day.
    c. He learned that the Count had gone away on a ship.
    d. The Count fed heavily (on Mina) the night before.

6. What happens as a result of Van Helsing's attempt to protect Mina from the Count while they are gone?
    a. She screams at the sight of a crucifix.
    b. Her forehead is badly burned and scarred.
    c. She cannot bear the smell of garlic and refuses to wear the flowers.
    d. She is insulted that he would think she was becoming a vampire.

Dracula Multiple Choice Questions Chapters 22-23 page 2

7. How does Van Helsing purify the boxes of earth at Carfax?
    a. He poured Holy Water on them.
    b. He placed a crucifix on each box.
    c. He places a piece of the Host in each box.
    d. He prayed the Lord's Prayer over each box.

8. What are the men distressed to learn about the boxes of earth at the Piccadilly house?
    a. The boxes have been locked.
    b. Six of the boxes are missing from the Piccadilly house.
    c. Seven of the boxes are still in the house, but two are missing
    d. Nine boxes were delivered to the house, but they only find eight.

9. What personal effects belonging to the Count do the men find a Piccadilly?
    a. deeds to property, keys to the houses, writing materials, personal hygiene items
    b. letters from Transylvania, books from his library
    c. jewelry and gem stones
    d. nothing

10. What physical changes have taken place in Jonathan Harker in the past twenty four hours?
    a. He has become more angry and determined to destroy the Count.
    b. He has become haggard, and his hair has turned white.
    c. He has become very pale and looks blood-less.
    d. He has a renewed sense of vigor because he wants to protect Mina.

11. What does Van Helsing learn of Count Dracula's mortal life?
    a. He was a prince in Turkey.
    b. He was a very religious man who lost his wife and became very bitter.
    c. He had been a king and had many servants.
    d. He had been a soldier, a statesman, and a brilliant alchemist.

12. What message is delivered to Van Helsing at the Piccadilly house?
    a. The lawyers have located other houses in London.
    b. The police have learned about the break in and are on their way.
    c. The Count has left Carfax and may be looking for them.
    d. The Count knows their plans and has left for Transylvania.

13. Who is the first to attempt to attack the Count upon Dracula's arrival at Piccadilly?
    a. Jonathan Harker
    b. Arthur
    c. Quincey Morris
    d. Van Helsing

Dracula Multiple Choice Questions Chapters 22-23 page 3

14. How does the Count escape capture from the group at Piccalilly?
    a. He knocks Van Helsing down and runs out past him.
    b. He jumps out the window.
    c. He turns to a mist and goes under the door.
    d. He turns into a bat and flies out the window.

15. What does the Count desperately attempt to take with him as he escaped from the house?
    a. his box of earth
    b. Mina Harker
    c. gold coins
    d. Jonathan's knife

16. What is the noise that Mina hears outside their bedroom in the night?
    a. Mina hears Lucy calling her name.
    b. Mina hears scratching on the bedroom door.
    c. Mina hears a child screaming for help.
    d. Mina hears Quincey Morris who is guarding their door.

17. What request does Mina make of Van Helsing?
    a. She asks him to protect Jonathan.
    b. She wants Van Helsing to hypnotize her.
    c. She wants Van Helsing to kill her and release her soul.
    d. She wants Van Helsing to read the Lord's prayer over her.

18. With what information is Mina able to supply Van Helsing?
    a. Under hypnosis, she is able to tell Van Helsing that the Count is on a boat.
    b. She is able to figure out precisely where the Count is headed.
    c. She knows where the last box of earth is hidden.
    d. She knows how to break the vampire's curse.

Chapters 24 and 25:

1. Where does Van Helsing believe that the Count is going?
    a. He believes the Count is going back to Carfax.
    b. He believes the Count is going to a new house in France.
    c. He believes the Count is going to Varna.
    d. He believes the Count is going home to Transylvania.

2. What news does the man from Doolittle's Wharf share with Van Helsing?
    a. He loaded several huge boxes onto a ship that already pulled out of the harbor.
    b. He booked passage for a tall, thin man with white teeth.
    c. Several of his employees have mysteriously disappeared.
    d. A large dog was seen lurking about the wharf for the last three nights.

3. Why does the Czarina Catherine not sail out on time?
    a. A sudden dense fog caused by the Count held up the departure.
    b. A sudden storm caused by the Count held up the departure.
    c. The main sail is torn while loading the Count's box.
    d. The inspector needs to review all the papers on the Count's box.

4. Why do Jonathan Harker and the others feel so compelled to follow the Count even though he is leaving the country?
    a. They want to avenge Lucy's death.
    b. They need to prove their theory about the Count.
    c. They believe the Count must be destroyed for the sake of humanity and Mina.
    d. Mina has begged them to kill the Count.

5. Explain Van Helsing's comparison of Dracula to a tiger.
    a. Once a tiger tastes human blood, it will always be a killer.
    b. Dracula has the strength of a tiger.
    c. A tiger hunts at night.
    d. Dracula is as cunning as a tiger.

6. What is a constant reminder that the events surrounding Dracula are real and not a dream?
    a. Jonathan Harker's journal of his adventures in Transylvania
    b. the reminder of how they destroyed the vampire Lucy
    c. Jonathan Harker's white hair
    d. the scar on Mina's forehead

7. Why does Van Helsing propose to keep Mina in the dark about the group's plans for the Count?
    a. He is afraid the stress is too much for Mina.
    b. He is afraid Dracula can read Mina's mind.
    c. He is afraid Mina will run to Dracula and tell him their plans.
    d. He is afraid Mina will sabotage their plans.

Dracula Multiple Choice Questions Chapters 24-25 page 2

8. What weapon(s) does Quincey Morris suggest the group should add to their arsenal?
   a. rosaries
   b. Holy Water
   c. Bowie knife
   d. Winchester rifle

9. What request does Mina make regarding the group's journey to follow the Count?
   a. She wants to go with them.
   b. She asks them to bring proof that the Count is really destroyed.
   c. She begs Jonathan to stay with her because she is frightened.
   d. She begs Van Helsing to watch over her husband for her.

10. What solemn promise does Mina ask of Jonathan and the other men?
    a. That no matter what happens, they will all remain friends.
    b. If she becomes a danger to them, that they will kill her and free her soul.
    c. If she becomes a danger, they will lock her away.
    d. If she dies, they will always keep fresh garlic flowers on her grave.

11. What does Mina ask Jonathan to read for her?
    a. She wants him to read his journal from Transylvania aloud to give him strength.
    b. She wants him to read the Burial Service for the Dead.
    c. She wants him to lead the men in reading the Lord's Prayer.
    d. She wants him to read from the Gospel according to John from the Bible.

12. What does Mina claim to hear when Van Helsing puts her into a hypnotic trance?
    a. Mina hears nothing at first, but then she hears waves lapping against a ship.
    b. Mina hears the Count calling her to come to him.
    c. Mina hears men shouting.
    d. Mina hears the maniacal laughter of Renfield.

13. Who or what is "Judge Money-bag" that Jonathan Harker refers to in his journal?
    a. It is bribery money.
    b. The lawyer at Lloyd's of London.
    c. The money the Count uses to buy passage back to Transylvania.
    d. The money Mina and Jonathan received from Mr. Hawkins.

14. What news do Van Helsing and the others receive about the Czarina Catherine?
    a. The ship ported at Galatz instead of at Varna.
    b. She helped the Count to escape to Transylvania.
    c. The ship was found at Varna completely empty like the Demeter in Whitby.
    d. The ship is lost at sea; no one has heard from it in weeks.

Dracula Multiple Choice Questions Chapters 24-25 page 3

15. How does the Count find out that Van Helsing and the others were chasing him?
    a. Czarina Catherine tells him.
    b. He changs into a bat and sees them pursuing him.
    c. His spies tell him.
    d. He is mentally linked to Mina, and he reads her mind.

16. What makes Van Helsing so absolutely certain that the Count is returning to his castle in Transylvania?
    a. The Count needs to return to Transylvania to get more boxes with dirt.
    b. When the Count is trouble he will return home as he has done in the past.
    c. The Count is going to Transylvania to bring the women back to London.
    d. When the Count jumped out the window, he lost all his money.

Chapters 26 and 27:

1. What does Van Helsing learn from Mina in her hypnotic state.?
    a. She hears waves lapping the side of the ship.
    b. She hears oars and there is a gleam of light and air blowing.
    c. She hears men and horses running.
    d. She hears nothing; she has lost her connection to the Count.

2. What seems to be happening to Mina's hypnotic trances?
    a. She is becoming more difficult to hypnotize.
    b. She is becoming violent under hypnosis and attacks Van Helsing.
    c. She is not able to come out of the trances easily once she is put under.
    d. She is refusing to be hypnotized; Van Helsing suspects that she is turning.

3. What had the Romanians on the crew of the Czarina Catherine requested several times of their captain?
    a. The Romanians requested more food.
    b. The Romanians wanted to leave the box at each port they passed.
    c. The Romanians wanted to throw the box overboard.
    d. The Romanians requested time to pray.

4. What becomes of Petrof Skinsky who has claimed the Count's box from the ship?
    a. He laughed in Van Helsing's face because the Count had outsmarted the men.
    b. After accepting a bribe, he told Van Helsing where the box was being taken.
    c. Petrof Skinsky never claimed the box; someone else did.
    d. He was found with his throat torn out.

5. What does Mina do for which Van Helsing and the others heartily congratulated her?
    a. She refused to give in to vampirism, even though she was strongly tempted.
    b. She logically figured out the route that Dracula was taking to his castle.
    c. She forced herself to eat a full meal with the men.
    d. She transcribed all of the journals with her typewriter to replace the burnt ones.

6. What single word does Mina hesitate to write in her journal?
    a. "drink"
    b. "pray"
    c. "death"
    d. "vampire"

Dracula Multiple Choice Questions Chapters 26-27 page 2

7. How does the group divide its members in order to best capture the Count?
    a. Arthur and Jonathan go by steamboat; Quincey and Dr. Seward go on horses; Mina and Van Helsing go straight to the castle.
    b. Arthur and Jonathan go on horses; Quincey and Dr. Seward go by steamboat; Mina and Van Helsing go straight to the castle.
    c. Arthur and Jonathan go by steamboat; the others wait in Varna.
    d. Mina and Van Helsing go by steamboat; the other go on horses.

8. How does Lord Godalming manage to trick boat owners to allow him to search their vessels along the river?
    a. He speaks fluent Romanian and he tells them that he is looking for a lost child.
    b. He flies the Romanian flag and boat owners assume he is a government official.
    c. He tells the boat owners that he is trying to break up a smuggling ring.
    d. He tells the boat owners that a madman has escaped and may be hiding aboard.

9. What seems to arouse the superstitions of the people that Van Helsing and Mina meet along their journey?
    a. They see Mina's scar.
    b. Van Helsing is wearing a garlic flower in his lapel.
    c. Van Helsing is asking too many questions about Castle Dracula.
    d. They see the marks on Mina's throat.

10. How has Mina's behavior changed since she and Van Helsing separated from the others?
    a. She is more relaxed and is getting stronger.
    b. She is very depressed.
    c. She is very weak and not sleeping.
    d. She is sleeping more, not writing in her journal, and knows the way to the Castle.

11. What precaution does Van Helsing take when he and Mina are forced to sleep outside for the night?
    a. He finds a cave so that he only has to worry about guarding them at the opening.
    b. He sleeps with a loaded rifle to keep wild animals away.
    c. He draws a circle around her and uses the Host to create a boundary.
    d. He creates a circle of salt around himself and Lucy.

12. What does Van Helsing see in the mist during the night?
    a. gleaming red eyes
    b. three voluptuous women
    c. wolves
    d. a large bat

Dracula Multiple Choice Questions Chapters 26-27 page 3

13. Although Mina is safe from vampires inside the circle, what other danger concerns Van Helsing?
    a. bats
    b. snow
    c. wolves
    d. Dracula's slaves

14. Van Helsing hesitates before killing the first vampire woman, what brings him back to his sense of purpose?
    a. He hears Mina wailing.
    b. He hears the Count calling to the women.
    c. He hears Jonathan yelling at him to kill them.
    d. He hears the women laughing at him.

15. What happens to each of the female vampires once Van Helsing has purified them?
    a. They scream obscenities at Van Helsing.
    b. They become old, grey, and wrinkled.
    c. They turn to dust.
    d. They try to seduce him one last time.

16. What does Van Helsing see through his field glass as he stood upon the large rock?
    a. He sees the carriage carrying the box and the men chasing after it.
    b. He sees the Count change into a bat.
    c. He sees the Count change into a wolf.
    d. He sees Jonathan stab the Count.

17. How is Count Dracula finally destroyed?
    a. Arthur cuts off his head while Quincey Morris drives a wooden stake in his heart. They then stuff his mouth with garlic.
    b. Dr. Seward, Quincey Morris, Arthur, and Jonathan surround him with holy objects. The Count is surrounded and turns to dust.
    c. The men open his box and expose him to the sun, which turns him to dust.
    d. Jonathan slits his throat while Quincey Morris stabs him in the chest.

18. What does **not** happen to members of the group after their terrible ordeal?
    a. Mina and Jonathan have a son and name him Quincey.
    b. Quincey survives his wounds.
    c. Van Helsing visits Mina and Jonathan.
    d. Dr. Seward and Arthur both marry.

ANSWER KEY - MULTIPLE CHOICE STUDY/QUIZ QUESTIONS
Dracula

	1-2	3-4	5-6	7-8	9-10	11-12	13-14	15-17	18-19	20-21	22-23	24-25	26-27
1	B	B	C	B	B	C	C	C	B	C	C	D	B
2	B	C	B	B	C	C	C	A	C	A	B	B	A
3	A	C	A	B	C	C	B	B	D	A	C	A	C
4	B	D	B	A	C	C	C	B	A	D	C	C	D
5	A	B	D	D	C	A	B	C	C	C	D	A	B
6	B	B	C	A	C	A	A	B	B	D	B	D	D
7	C	A	A	C	B	A	A	C	C	A	C	B	A
8	B	A	B	D	D	B	C	B	D	C	D	D	B
9	D	D	B	A	C	A	A	D	D	B	A	A	A
10	C	C	D	C	D	B	B	C	B	A	B	B	D
11	B	B		C	B	B	B	A	C	D	D	B	C
12	B	C		B	C	A	A	C	D	B	C	C	B
13	C	C		A	D	C	B	B	D	C	A	A	C
14	A	B		C	D		B	A	B	A	B	A	A
15	A	B		A	A		B	D	A	B	C	D	C
16		D		A			B	A	B	C	D	B	A
17		B		A				B	D		B		D
18		A						B			A		B
19								D					
20								A					
21								B					
22								A					
23								B					
24								C					
25								A					

PREREADING VOCABULARY WORKSHEETS

VOCABULARY CHAPTERS 1-2 *Dracula*

Part I: Using Prior Knowledge and Contextual Clues

Below are the sentences in which the vocabulary words appear in the text. Read the sentence. Use any clues you can find in the sentence combined with your prior knowledge, and write what you think the underlined words mean on the lines provided.

1. "The strangest figures we saw were the Slovaks… On the stage they would be set down at once as some old Oriental band of **brigands**."

2. "…on making inquiries as to details he seemed somewhat **reticent**, and pretended that he could not understand my German."

3. "I could hear a lot of words often repeated…; so I got my **polyglot** dictionary from my bag and looked them out."

4. "Then, amongst a chorus of screams from the peasants and a universal crossing of themselves, a **caleche** with four horses drove up behind us…"

5. "Give me the Herr's luggage," said the driver; and with exceeding **alacrity** my bags were handed out and put on the caleche."

6. "Again I could not but notice his **prodigious** strength. His hand actually seemed like a steel vice that could have crushed mine if he had chosen."

7. "The light and warmth and the Count's courteous welcome seemed to have **dissipated** all my doubts and fears."

8. "I much regret that an attack of gout, from which **malady** I am a constant sufferer, forbids me absolutely any traveling on my part for some time to come…"

Dracula Vocabulary Worksheet Chapters 1-2 Continued

9. "Come…tell me of London and of the house that you have **procured** for me."

_____

10. "…his cast of face made his smile look malignant and **saturnine**."

_____

Part II: Determining the Meaning
  Match the vocabulary words to their dictionary definitions

___ 1. brigands   A. impressively great in size, force, or extent; enormous
___ 2. reticent   B. a light carriage with two or four low wheels and a collapsible top
___ 3. polyglot   C. inclined to keep one's thoughts, feelings, and personal affairs to oneself
___ 4. caleche   D. drove away; dispersed
___ 5. alacrity   E. robbers or bandits, especially of an outlaw band
___ 6. prodigious   F. got by special effort; obtained or acquired
___ 7. dissipated   G. speaking, writing, written in, or composed of several languages
___ 8. malady   H. cheerful willingness; eagerness; speed or quickness
___ 9. procured   I. melancholy or sullen; having or marked by a tendency to be bitter
___ 10. saturnine   J. a disease, a disorder, or an ailment

VOCABULARY CHAPTERS 3-4 *Dracula*

Part I: Using Prior Knowledge and Contextual Clues

Below are the sentences in which the vocabulary words appear in the text. Read the sentence. Use any clues you can find in the sentence combined with your prior knowledge, and write what you think the underlined words mean on the lines provided.

1. "…if he does himself all these **menial** offices, surely it is proof that there is no one else to do them."

2. "Now, suppose I…wish to ship goods…to Newcastle, or Durham, or Harwich, or Dover, might it not be that it could with more ease be done by **consigning** to one in these ports?"

3. "For a man who was never in the country, and who did not evidently do much in the way of business, his knowledge and **acumen** were wonderful."

4. "The castle was built on the corner of a great rock, so that on three sides it was quite **impregnable**."

5. "All three had brilliant white teeth, that shone like pearls against the ruby of their **voluptuous** lips."

6. "I closed my eyes in a **languorous** ecstasy and waited – waited with a beating heart."

7. "They took their hats off and made **obeisance** and many signs, which, however, I could not understand any more than I could their spoken language…"

8. "This morning, as I was sitting on the edge of my bed **cudgeling** my brains, I heard without a crack of whips and pounding and scraping of horses' feet up the rocky path beyond the courtyard."

Dracula Vocabulary Worksheet Chapters 3-4 Continued

9. "I leaned back in the **embrasure** in a more comfortable position, so that I could enjoy myself more fully in the aerial gamboling."

_____

10. "Suddenly it struck me that this might be the moment and the means of my doom; I was to be given to the wolves, and at my own **instigation**."

_____

Part II: Determining the Meaning
    Match the vocabulary words to their dictionary definitions

___ 1. menial	A.	deliberate and intentional triggering of trouble or discord
___ 2. consigning	B.	arising from or contributing to the satisfaction of sensual desires
___ 3. acumen	C.	relating to work or a job regarded as for a servant
___ 4. impregnable	D.	beating or striking as if with a heavy stick
___ 5. voluptuous	E.	give over to the care of another; entrust
___ 6. languorous	F.	lack of physical or mental energy; listlessness
___ 7. obeisance	G.	quickness, accuracy, and keenness of judgment or insight
___ 8. cudgeling	H.	impossible to capture or enter by force
___ 9. embrasure	I.	an opening in a thick wall for a window, often containing a bench
___ 10. instigation	J.	gesture, such as a curtsy, that expresses deference or respect

VOCABULARY CHAPTERS 5-6 *Dracula*

Part I: Using Prior Knowledge and Contextual Clues

Below are the sentences in which the vocabulary words appear in the text. Read the sentence. Use any clues you can find in the sentence combined with your prior knowledge, and write what you think the underlined words mean on the lines provided.

1. "…I want to keep up with Jonathan's studies, and I have been practicing shorthand very **assiduously**."

2. "I think he is one of the most resolute men I ever saw, and yet the most calm. He seems absolutely **imperturbable**."

3. "…before I could say a word, he began pouring out a perfect **torrent** of lovemaking, laying his very heart and soul at my feet."

4. "I presume that the **sanguine** temperament itself and the disturbing influence end in a mentally accomplished finish; a possible dangerous man, probably dangerous if unselfish."

5. "A great **viaduct** runs across [over a deep valley], with high piers, through which the view seems somehow further away than it really is."

6. "Even my old man **succumbed** and did not contradict her, but gave me double share instead."

7. "He has at present such a quantity [of flies] that I have had myself to **expostulate**."

8. "…I said that he must clear out some of them, at all events. He cheerfully **acquiesced** in this, and I gave him some time as before for reduction."

Dracula Vocabulary Worksheet Chapters 5-6 Continued

9. "My friend has now a whole colony of sparrows, and his flies and spiders are almost **obliterated**."

_____

10. "Men sneered at **vivisection**, and yet look at its results today!"

_____

Part II: Determining the Meaning
    Match the vocabulary words to their dictionary definitions

____ 1. assiduously   A. bridge consisting of arches used to carry a road over a valley
____ 2. imperturbable   B. with care and persistence
____ 3. torrent   C. to consent or comply passively or without protest
____ 4. sanguine   D. yielded to an overwhelming desire; gave up or gave in
____ 5. viaduct   E. to do away with completely so as to leave no trace
____ 6. succumbed   F. cheerfully confident; optimistic; of a healthy reddish color
____ 7. expostulate   G. injuring living animals for the purpose of scientific research
____ 8. acquiesced   H. a heavy, uncontrolled outpouring
____ 9. obliterated   I. to reason with someone in an effort to dissuade or correct
____ 10. vivisection   J. unshakably calm and collected

VOCABULARY CHAPTERS 7-8 *Dracula*

Part I: Using Prior Knowledge and Contextual Clues

Below are the sentences in which the vocabulary words appear in the text. Read the sentence. Use any clues you can find in the sentence combined with your prior knowledge, and write what you think the underlined words mean on the lines provided.

1. "The day was unusually fine till the afternoon, when some of the gossips who frequent the East Cliff churchyard, and from that commanding **eminence** watch the wide sweep of the sea…called attention to a sudden show of 'mares'-tails' high in the sky…"

2. "The foolhardiness or ignorance of her officers was a **prolific** theme for comment whilst she remained in sight…"

3. "In his pocket was a bottle, carefully corked, empty save for a little roll of paper, which proved to be an **addendum** to the log."

4. "Four days in hell, knocking about in a sort of **maelstrom**, and the wind of a tempest."

5. "There is no evidence to **adduce**; and whether or no the man himself committed the murders there is now none to say."

6. The whole **agglomeration** of things—the ship steered into port by a dead man, …, the touching funeral, the dog, now furious and now in terror—will afford material for her dreams."

7. "I think someday the bishops must get together and see about breeding up a new class of **curates**, who don't take supper, no matter how they may be pressed to…"

8. "There was a bright full moon, with heavy black, driving clouds, which threw the whole scene into a fleeting **diorama** of light and shade as they sailed across."

Dracula Vocabulary Worksheet Chapters 7-8 Continued

9. "Lucy was **languid** and tired, and slept on after we had been called."

_____

10. "I thought I would find out if his **apathy** were real or only assumed, and tried to lead him to talk of his pets, a theme which had never failed to excite his attention."

_____

Part II: Determining the Meaning
  Match the vocabulary words to their dictionary definitions

  ___ 1. eminence
  ___ 2. prolific
  ___ 3. addendum
  ___ 4. maelstrom
  ___ 5. adduce
  ___ 6. agglomeration
  ___ 7. curates
  ___ 8. diorama
  ___ 9. languid
  ___ 10. apathy

  A. to cite as an example or means of proof in an argument
  B. something added or to be added, as in a supplement to a book
  C. lack of interest or concern, lack of emotion or feeling
  D. a position of great distinction or superiority
  E. a cleric, especially one who has charge of a parish
  F. lacking energy or vitality; weak
  G. producing abundant works or results
  H. a violent or turbulent situation: a large violent whirlpool
  I. a confused or jumbled mass
  J. scene in which figures are arranged in a naturalistic setting against a painted background

VOCABULARY CHAPTERS 9-10 *Dracula*

Part I: Using Prior Knowledge and Contextual Clues

Below are the sentences in which the vocabulary words appear in the text. Read the sentence. Use any clues you can find in the sentence combined with your prior knowledge, and write what you think the underlined words mean on the lines provided.

1. "…the ravings of the sick were the secrets of God, and that if a nurse through her **vocation** should hear them, she should respect her trust."

   _____

2. "I have an appetite like a **cormorant**, am full of life and sleep well."

   _____

3. "…at last he fell into a **paroxysm** which exhausted him so that he swooned into a sort of coma."

   _____

4. "I told her I should ask you to see her, and though she **demurred** at first,… she finally consented."

   _____

5. "…Lucy was left with me. We went into her **boudoir**, and till we got there her gaiety remained…"

   _____

6. "But you do not find the good husbandman dig up his planted corn to see if he grow; that is for the children who play at **husbandry**, and not for those who take it as of work for their life."

   _____

7. "Van Helsing's face grew set as marble, and his eyebrows **converged** till they almost touched over his nose."

   _____

8. "…but now, as he took in his **stalwart** proportions and recognized the strong young manhood which seemed to emanate from him, his eyes gleamed."

   _____

Dracula Vocabulary Worksheet Chapters 9-10 Continued

9. "There was no sign of disease, but the edges were white and worn-looking, as if by some **trituration**."

_____

10. "Ah, not if you were like me—if sleep was to you a **presage** of horror!"

_____

Part II: Determining the Meaning
   Match the vocabulary words to their dictionary definitions

   ___ 1. vocation   A. voiced opposition; objected
   ___ 2. cormorant   B. a sudden outburst of emotion or action
   ___ 3. paroxysm   C. an occupation, especially one for which a person is suited
   ___ 4. demurred   D. came together from different directions; met
   ___ 5. boudoir   E. bruising or crushing
   ___ 6. husbandry   F. a greedy, rapacious person
   ___ 7. converged   G. an indication or warning of a future occurrence; an omen
   ___ 8. stalwart   H. the practice of growing crops, breeding and raising livestock
   ___ 9. trituration   I. having or marked by imposing physical strength
   ___ 10. presage   J. a woman's private sitting room, dressing room, or bedroom

VOCABULARY CHAPTERS 11-12 *Dracula*

Part I: Using Prior Knowledge and Contextual Clues

Below are the sentences in which the vocabulary words appear in the text. Read the sentence. Use any clues you can find in the sentence combined with your prior knowledge, and write what you think the underlined words mean on the lines provided.

1. "This time he did not start as he looked on the poor face with the same awful, waxen pallor as before."

   _____

2. "I have a dim half-remembrance in which there was not even the pain of hope to make present distress more **poignant**…"

   _____

3. "How do you mean, ask them questions?" I **queried**, wishful to get him into a talkative humour."

   _____

4. "I couldn't cope in **badinage** with the worthy Thomas, but I thought I knew a surer way to his heart…"

   _____

5. "If he doesn't, and some nursemaid goes a-walkin' orf with a soldier, leavin' of the infant in the **perambulator**—well then I shouldn't be surprised if the census is one baby the less."

   _____

6. "Hitherto I had blamed only the servants, but now a terrible fear began to **assail** me."

   _____

7. "There was no need to think them dead, for their **stertorous** breathing and the acrid smell of laudanum in the room left no debate as to their condition."

   _____

8. "However, the action of both heart and lungs improved, and Van Helsing made a **subcutaneous** injection of morphia, as before, and with good effect."

   _____

Dracula Vocabulary Worksheet Chapters 11-12 Continued

9. "...even now he sometimes starts out of his sleep in a sudden way and awakes all trembling until I can coax him back to his usual **placidity**."

_____

10. "...the dear, good man...has treated him like his own son and left him a fortune which to people of our modest bringing up is wealth beyond the dream of **avarice**..."

_____

Part II: Determining the Meaning
    Match the vocabulary words to their dictionary definitions

    ___ 1. pallor   A. immoderate desire for wealth; greed
    ___ 2. poignant   B. a heavy snoring sound in respiration
    ___ 3. queried   C. undisturbed by tumult or disorder; relaxation
    ___ 4. badinage   D. to attack, as with ridicule
    ___ 5. perambulator   E. uestioned; inquired
    ___ 6. assail   F. light, playful banter
    ___ 7. stertorous   G. distressing to the mind or feelings; profoundly moving or touching
    ___ 8. subcutaneous   H. located or placed just beneath the skin
    ___ 9. placidity   I. extreme or unnatural paleness
    ___ 10. avarice   J. a baby carriage

VOCABULARY CHAPTERS 13-14 *Dracula*

Part I: Using Prior Knowledge and Contextual Clues

Below are the sentences in which the vocabulary words appear in the text. Read the sentence. Use any clues you can find in the sentence combined with your prior knowledge, and write what you think the underlined words mean on the lines provided.

1. "I attended to all the ghastly formalities, and the **urbane** undertaker proved that his staff were afflicted—or blessed—with something of his own obsequious suavity."

   _____

2. "…he informed us that, with the exception of certain **entailed** property of Lucy's father's, …the whole estate…was left to Arthur Holmwood."

   _____

3. "It frightened and amazed me somewhat; and as for Arthur, he fell a-trembling, and finally was shaken with doubt as with an **ague**."

   _____

4. "I felt it very improper, for you can't go on for years teaching etiquette and decorum to other girls without the **pedantry** of it biting into yourself a bit…"

   _____

5. "And yet I can laugh at her very grave—laugh when the clay from the spade of the **sexton** drop upon her coffin…"

   _____

6. "It was terribly weak and looked quite **emaciated**."

   _____

7. "Here was a rare interview; I shall try to record it **verbatim**."

   _____

8. "The pity of Jonathan, the horror which he experienced, the whole fearful mystery of his diary, and the fear that has been brooding over me ever since, all came in a **tumult**."

   _____

Dracula Vocabulary Worksheet Chapters 13-14 Continued

9. It was the doubt as to the reality of the whole thing that knocked me over. I felt **impotent**, and in the dark, and distrustful."

_____

10. "No, you don't; you couldn't with eyebrows like yours."
    "So! You are **physiognomist**. I learn more here with each hour."

_____

Part II: Determining the Meaning
    Match the vocabulary words to their dictionary definitions

    ___ 1. urbane   A. extremely thin, especially as a result of starvation
    ___ 2. entailed   B. polite, refined, and often elegant in manner
    ___ 3. ague   C. in exactly the same words; word for word
    ___ 4. pedantry   D. limited inheritance of property to specified heirs
    ___ 5. sexton   E. agitation of the mind or emotions
    ___ 6. emaciated   F. a chill or fit of shivering
    ___ 7. verbatim   G. lacking physical strength or vigor; weak
    ___ 8. tumult   H. an inappropriate display of learning
    ___ 9. impotent   I. one who judges human character from facial features
    ___ 10. physiognomist   J. an employee responsible for the upkeep of church property

VOCABULARY CHAPTERS 15-17 *Dracula*

Part I: Using Prior Knowledge and Contextual Clues

Below are the sentences in which the vocabulary words appear in the text. Read the sentence. Use any clues you can find in the sentence combined with your prior knowledge, and write what you think the underlined words mean on the lines provided.

1. "I **smote** the table hard and rose up as I said, "Dr. Van Helsing, are you mad?"

_____

2. "…I realized distinctly the perils of the law which we were incurring in out **unhallowed** work"

_____

3. "Van Helsing did not seem to notice my silence; at any rate, he showed neither **chagrin** nor triumph."

_____

4. "Me, too," said Quincey Morris **laconically**.

_____

5. "I had myself been apprenticed by my former visits to this watching horror; and yet I, who had up to an hour ago **repudiated** the proofs, felt my heart sink within me."

_____

6. "We shuddered with horror. I could see by the **tremulous** light that even Van Helsing's iron nerve had failed."

_____

7. "Then our promise shall be made to each other anew; for there is a terrible task before us, and once our feet are on the **ploughshare**, we must not draw back."

_____

8. "When I have returned you will be master of all the facts, and we can then better enter on our **inquisition**."

_____

Dracula Vocabulary Worksheet Chapters 15-17 Continued

9. "The blush that rose to my own cheeks somehow set us both at ease, for it was a **tacit** answer to her own [blush]."

_____

10. "Fortunately, I am not of a fainting **disposition**."

_____

Part II: Determining the Meaning
   Match the vocabulary words to their dictionary definitions

___ 1. smote   A. using or marked by the use of few words; terse or concise
___ 2. unhallowed   B. strong feelings of embarrassment
___ 3. chagrin   C. one's usual mood; temperament
___ 4. laconically   D. a sharp steel wedge that cuts loose the top layer of soil
___ 5. repudiated   E. rejected emphatically as unfounded, untrue, or unjust
___ 6. tremulous   F. marked by trembling, quivering, or shaking
___ 7. ploughshare   G. unholy
___ 8. inquisition   H. to strike down or hit
___ 9. tacit   I. not spoken
___ 10. disposition J. the act of inquiring into a matter; an investigation

VOCABULARY CHAPTERS 18-19 *Dracula*

Part I: Using Prior Knowledge and Contextual Clues

Below are the sentences in which the vocabulary words appear in the text. Read the sentence. Use any clues you can find in the sentence combined with your prior knowledge, and write what you think the underlined words mean on the lines provided.

1. "Since I myself have been an inmate of a lunatic asylum, I cannot but notice that the **sophistic** tendencies of some of its inmates lean towards the errors of *non causae* and *ignoratio elenchi*."

   _____

2. "...I tried to kill him for the purpose of strengthening my vital powers by the **assimilation** with my own body of his life through the medium of his blood..."

   _____

3. "In fact, so far as our powers extend, they are **unfettered**, and we are free to use them."

   _____

4. "Then there are things which so **afflict** him that he has no power, as the garlic that we know of..."

   _____

5. "He moved towards me so quickly that for the moment I feared that he was about to make another **homicidal** attack."

   _____

6. "...'put these flowers round your neck'—here he handed me a wreath of withered garlic blossoms—'for other enemies more **mundane**, this revolver and this knife...'"

   _____

7. "We were prepared for some unpleasantness, for as we were opening the door a faint, **malodorous** air seemed to exhale through the gaps..."

   _____

8. "One lesson, too, we have learned...: that the brute beasts which are to the Count's command are yet themselves not **amenable** to his spiritual power..."

   _____

Dracula Vocabulary Worksheet Chapters 18-19 Continued

9. "They all agreed that it was best that I should not be drawn further into this awful work, and I **acquiesced**."

_____

10. "I was not so sleepy as I should have been; so before they went I asked Dr. Seward to give me a little **opiate** of some kind, as I had not slept well the night before."

_____

Part II: Determining the Meaning
    Match the vocabulary words to their dictionary definitions

    ____ 1. sophistic   A. responsive to advice, authority, or suggestion; willing
    ____ 2. assimilation   B. something that dulls the senses and induces relaxation
    ____ 3. unfettered   C. to set free or keep free from restrictions or bonds
    ____ 4. afflict   D. adopting the customs and attitudes of the prevailing culture
    ____ 5. homicidal   E. murderous
    ____ 6. mundane   F. having a bad odor; foul
    ____ 7. malodorous   G. to inflict grievous physical or mental suffering on
    ____ 8. amenable   H. to consent or comply passively or without protest
    ____ 9. acquiesced   I. relating to commonplace things; ordinary
    ____ 10. opiate   J. characteristics of a scholar or thinker

VOCABULARY CHAPTERS 20-21 *Dracula*

Part I: Using Prior Knowledge and Contextual Clues

Below are the sentences in which the vocabulary words appear in the text. Read the sentence. Use any clues you can find in the sentence combined with your prior knowledge, and write what you think the underlined words mean on the lines provided.

1. "The very prospect of beer which my expected coming had opened to him had proved too much, and he had begun too early on his expected **debauch**."

_____

2. "I came across the house described, and was satisfied that this was the next of the **lairs** arranged by Dracula."

_____

3. "Mina was looking tired and pale, but she made a gallant effort to be bright and cheerful; it wrung my heart to think that I had to keep anything from her and so caused her **inquietude**."

_____

4. "I could not at the moment recall Enoch's **appositeness**; so I had to ask a simple question, though I felt that by doing so I was lowering myself in the eyes of the lunatic—"

_____

5. "If we could only get some hint as to what passed in his mind, between the time of my argument with him today and his **resumption** of fly-catching, it might afford us a valuable clue."

_____

6. "Van Helsing returned with extraordinary **celerity**, bearing with him a surgical case."

_____

7. "Her face was ghastly, with a pallor which was **accentuated** by the blood which smeared her lips and cheeks and chin; from her throat trickled a thin stream of blood."

_____

8. "Then she raised her head proudly, and held out one hand to Van Helsing who took it in his, and, after stooping and kissing it **reverently**, held it fast."

_____

Dracula Vocabulary Worksheet Chapters 20-21 Continued

9. "Whilst they played wits against me—against me who commanded nations, and **intrigued** for them, and fought for them, hundreds of years before they were born—I was countermining them."

_____

10. "But as yet you are to be punished for what you have done. You have aided in **thwarting** me; now you shall come to my call."

_____

Part II: Determining the Meaning
    Match the vocabulary words to their dictionary definitions

    ____ 1. debauch   A. the den or dwelling of a wild animal; a hideaway
    ____ 2. lairs   B. beginning again
    ____ 3. inquietude   C. engaged in secret or underhanded schemes; spied
    ____ 4. appositeness   D. in a state of profound awe and respect and often love
    ____ 5. resumption   E. to corrupt morally
    ____ 6. celerity   F. swiftness of action or motion; speed
    ____ 7. accentuated   G. opposing and defeating the efforts, plans, or ambitions of something
    ____ 8. reverently   H. to stress or emphasize; intensify
    ____ 9. intrigued   I. a state of restlessness or uneasiness
    ____ 10. thwarting   J. strikingly appropriate and relevant

VOCABULARY CHAPTERS 22-23 *Dracula*

Part I: Using Prior Knowledge and Contextual Clues

Below are the sentences in which the vocabulary words appear in the text. Read the sentence. Use any clues you can find in the sentence combined with your prior knowledge, and write what you think the underlined words mean on the lines provided.

1. "…don't you think that one of your snappy carriages with its **heraldic** adornments in a bye way of Walworth or Mile End would attract too much attention for our purposes?"

_____

2. "But the words to her thought came quickly; the echo of the scream had not ceased to ring on the air when there came the reaction, and she sank on her knees on the floor in an agony of **abasement**."

_____

3. "It was hard to believe that amongst so **prosaic** surroundings of neglect and dust and decay there was any ground for the fear as already we knew."

_____

4. "I demurred as to my not sharing any danger even of **odium**…"

_____

5. "We moved to explore the house, all keeping together in case of attack; for we knew we had a strong and **wily** enemy to deal with…"

_____

6. "Today he is a drawn, **haggard** old man, whose white hair matches well with the hollow burning eyes and grief written lines of his face."

_____

7. "The boy handed in a **despatch**. The Professor closed the door again and, after looking at the direction, opened it and read it aloud."

_____

8. "…Quincey Morris had always been the one to arrange the plan of action, and Arthur and I had been accustomed to obey him **implicitly**."

_____

Dracula Vocabulary Worksheet Chapters 22-23 Continued

9. "A second less and the **trenchant** blade had shorne through his heart."

_____

10. "It would be impossible to describe the expression of hate and baffled **malignity**—of anger and hellish rage—which came over the Count's face."

_____

Part II: Determining the Meaning
   Match the vocabulary words to their dictionary definitions

____ 1. heraldic   A. matter-of-fact; straightforward; lacking imagination; dull
____ 2. abasement   B. forceful, effective, and vigorous
____ 3. prosaic   C. a low or downcast state
____ 4. odium   D. strong dislike, contempt, or aversion
____ 5. wily   E. written official message sent with speed
____ 6. haggard   F. intense ill will or hatred; great malice
____ 7. despatch   G. marked by skill in deception
____ 8. implicitly   H. indicative of or announcing something to come
____ 9. trenchant   I. appearing worn and exhausted
____ 10. malignity   J. in a manner which is understood though not directly expressed

VOCABULARY CHAPTERS 24-25 *Dracula*

Part I: Using Prior Knowledge and Contextual Clues

Below are the sentences in which the vocabulary words appear in the text. Read the sentence. Use any clues you can find in the sentence combined with your prior knowledge, and write what you think the underlined words mean on the lines provided.

1. "He is **finite**, though he is powerful to do much harm and suffers not as we do."

2. "There are deep caverns and **fissures** that reach none known whither."

3. "There have been volcanoes, some of whose openings still send out waters of strange properties, and gases that kill or make to **vivify**."

4. "Well, there may be a poison that **distils** itself out of good things; in an age when the existence of ptomaines is a mystery we should not wonder at anything!"

5. "I know that if he tells me to come in secret, I must come by wile; by any device to **hoodwink** —even Jonathan."

6. "Tonight, when we met she was somewhat **constrained**, and bore all the signs of internal struggle."

7. "We were all silent, for we knew instinctively that this was only a **prelude**. The faces of the others were set, and Harker's grew ashen grey; perhaps he guessed better than any of us what was coming."

8. "'Again I swear!' came the Professor's **resonant** voice."

Dracula Vocabulary Worksheet Chapters 24-25 Continued

9. "To write diary with a pen is **irksome** to me, but Van Helsing says I must."

___

10. "Van Helsing raised his hands over his head for a moment, as though in **remonstrance** with the Almighty; but he said not a word, and in a few seconds stood up with his face sternly set."

___

Part II: Determining the Meaning
    Match the vocabulary words to their dictionary definitions

___ 1. finite   A. long narrow opening; a crack or cleft
___ 2. fissures   B. having bounds; limited
___ 3. vivify   C. causing annoyance, weariness, or vexation
___ 4. distils   D. to give or bring life to
___ 5. hoodwink   E. strong and deep in tone
___ 6. constrained   F. separates or purifies
___ 7. prelude   G. in a forced or inhibited manner
___ 8. resonant   H. an expression of protest or complaint
___ 9. irksome   I. to take in by deceptive means; deceive
___ 10. remonstrance   J. introductory event or action preceding a more important one

VOCABULARY CHAPTERS 26-27 *Dracula*

Part I: Using Prior Knowledge and Contextual Clues

Below are the sentences in which the vocabulary words appear in the text. Read the sentence. Use any clues you can find in the sentence combined with your prior knowledge, and write what you think the underlined words mean on the lines provided.

1. "If I thought that the Count's power over her would die away…it would be a happy thought; but I am afraid that it may not be so. When she did speak, her words were **enigmatical**."

2. "When Skinsky had come to him, he had taken him to the ship and handed over the box, so as to save **porterage**."

3. "…he evidently intended to arrive at Galatz, and sent invoice to Varna to deceive us lest we should **ascertain** his means of exit from England…"

4. "The Count, if you remember, took some other precautions; [Mr. Morris] made some **requisitions** on others that Mrs. Harker could not quite hear or understand."

5. "With every boat which we have overhauled since this trick has succeeded; we have had **deference** shown to us, and not once any objection to whatever we chose to ask or do."

6. "Presently the horses began to scream, and tore at their **tethers** till I came to them and quieted them."

7. "I was **desolate** and afraid, and full of woe and terror; but when that beautiful sun began to climb the horizon life was to me again."

8. "The evening was now drawing close, and well I knew that at sunset the Thing, which was till then imprisoned there, would take new freedom and could in any of many forms **elude** all pursuit."

Dracula Vocabulary Worksheet Chapters 26-27 Continued

9. "When the snowstorm **abated** a moment we looked again."

_____

10. "And, to our bitter grief, with a smile and in silence, he died, a **gallant** gentleman."

_____

Part II: Determining the Meaning
   Match the vocabulary words to their dictionary definitions

____ 1. enigmatical	A. yielding to the opinion, wishes, or judgment of another
____ 2. porterage	B. reduced in amount, degree, or intensity
____ 3. ascertain	C. unflinching in battle or action; valiant
____ 4. requisitions	D. restraint for holding an animal in place
____ 5. deference	E. to evade or escape from, as by daring, cleverness, or skill
____ 6. tether	F. barren; lifeless
____ 7. desolate	G. to make certain, definite, and precise
____ 8. elude	H. formal written requests for something needed
____ 9. abated	I. charge for the carrying of burdens or goods as done by porters
____ 10. gallant	J. puzzling or mysterious

VOCABULARY ANSWER KEY
Dracula

	1-2	3-4	5-6	7-8	9-10	11-12	13-14	15-17	18-19	20-21	22-23	24-25	26-27
1	E	C	B	D	C	I	B	H	J	E	H	B	J
2	C	E	J	G	F	G	D	G	D	A	C	A	I
3	G	G	H	B	B	E	F	B	C	I	A	D	G
4	B	H	F	H	A	F	H	A	G	J	D	F	H
5	H	B	A	A	J	J	J	E	E	B	G	I	A
6	A	F	D	I	H	D	A	F	I	F	I	G	D
7	D	J	I	E	D	B	C	D	F	H	E	J	F
8	J	D	C	J	I	H	E	J	A	D	J	E	E
9	F	I	E	F	E	C	G	I	H	C	B	C	B
10	I	A	G	C	G	A	I	C	B	G	F	H	C

DAILY LESSONS

LESSON ONE

Objectives
1. To become familiar with the elements of the Gothic Literature genre
2. To become familiar with Bram Stoker, the author of *Dracula*
3. To introduce the *Dracula* unit
4. To distribute books, study guides, and other related materials
5. To preview the vocabulary worksheet and study guide questions for chapters 1-2
6. To read chapters 1-2
7. To evaluate students oral reading

Activity #1

Ask students to brainstorm what makes a good ghost/horror story; they should list at least three elements that should be included. Students share ideas aloud and write them on the chalk board. For any of the elements they may have missed (see list on page 115), ask leading questions so that students can come up with the answers themselves.

Activity #2

Give brief notes about the life of Bram Stoker (see A Few Notes About The Author), and discuss how certain aspects of his life might have lead him to write in the Gothic Horror genre. Also, read aloud the story "Dracula's Guest" which was originally the first chapter of his novel *Dracula*; it was deleted from the novel because of the novel's length. It can be found on the Internet, but any gothic tale will do for this exercise. (SUGGESTIONS: any short story by Edgar Allan Poe, "Dagon" or "In the Vault" by H. P. Lovecraft. "Dr. Heidegger's Experiment" by Nathaniel Hawthorne, "Markheim" by Robert Louis Stevenson) Discuss what elements of the gothic genre from the front board can be found in this story.

Activity #3

Distribute the materials students will use in this unit. Explain in detail how students are to use these materials.

Study Guides   Students should read the study guide questions for each reading assignment prior to beginning the reading assignment to get a feeling for what events and ideas are important in the section they are about to read. After reading the section, students will (as a class or individually) answer the questions to review the important events and ideas from that section of the book. Students should keep the study guides as study materials for the unit test.

Vocabulary   Prior to each reading assignment, students will do vocabulary work related to the section of the book they are about to read. Following the completion of the reading of the book, there will be a vocabulary review of all the words used in the vocabulary assignments. Students should keep their vocabulary work as study materials for the unit test.

Reading Assignment Sheet   You need to fill in the reading assignment sheet to let students know by when their reading has to be completed. You can either write the assignment sheet up on a side blackboard or bulletin board and leave it there for students to see each day, or you can photocopy schedules for each student to have. In either case, you should advise students to become very familiar with the reading assignments so they know what is expected of them.

<u>Extra Activities Center</u> The Unit Resource Materials portion of this LitPlan contains suggestions for an extra library of related books and articles in your classroom as well as crossword and word search puzzles. Make an extra activities center in your room where you will keep these materials for students to use. (Bring the books and articles in from the library and keep several copies of the puzzles on hand.) Explain to students that these materials are available for students to use when they finish reading assignments or other class work early.

<u>Nonfiction Assignment Sheet</u> Explain to students that they each are to read at least one non-fiction piece from the in-class library at some time during the unit. Students will fill out a nonfiction assignment sheet after completing the reading to help you (the teacher) evaluate their reading experiences and to help the students think about and evaluate their own reading experiences.

<u>Books</u> Each school has its own rules and regulations regarding student use of school books. Advise students of the procedures that are normal for your school. Preview the book. Look at the covers, front-matter, and index.

<u>Activity #4</u>

Have students look at and read through the study questions for chapters 1-2. This can be done silently or orally.

<u>Activity #5</u>

Do the first vocabulary worksheet (for chapters 1-2) orally, together as a class, to show students how the vocabulary worksheets should be done prior to each reading assignment.

<u>Activity #6</u>

Have students read chapters 1-2 of *Dracula* out loud in class. You probably know the best way to get readers with your class; pick students at random, ask for volunteers, or use whatever method works best for your group. If you have not yet completed an oral reading evaluation for your students this period, this would be a good opportunity to do so. A form is included with this unit for your convenience. If time runs out in class, students should do this assignment as homework and have it completed prior to the next class period.

Gothic literature contains a combination of several of these elements:

- a deserted (or sparsely inhabited) castle or mansion in a state of ruins or semi-ruins

- labyrinths/mazes, dark corridors, and winding stairs filled with dusty cobwebs

- these castles or mansions have hidden tunnels/staircases, dungeons, underground passages, crypts, or catacombs

- if set in a broken down modern house, the basement or attic becomes the place of terror

- limited lighting such as moonlight (usually a full moon), candles, flashlight, lantern; often the light disappears: clouds hide the moon, candles go out, flashlights/lanterns are dropped and broken

- if electric lights exist, they usually mysteriously go out

- the setting is usually threatening natural landscapes, like rugged mountains, dark forests, or eerie moors, exhibiting stormy weather

- dark secrets surrounding some tormented soul who is left to live in isolation

- ominous omens and curses

- magic, supernatural manifestations, or the suggestion of the supernatural

- a damsel in distress

- the damsel's rescuer; usually a lover

- horrifying (or terrifying) events or the threat of such happenings

LESSON TWO

Objectives
1. To review the main events and ideas from chapters 1-2
2. To distribute non-fiction assignment about 19th century concepts and ideas
3. To evaluate students' oral reading
4. To preview the study guide questions and vocabulary for Chapters 3-4
5. To read chapters 3-4

Activity #1
Give students a few minutes to formulate answers for the study guide questions for Chapters 1-2, and then discuss the answers to the questions in detail. Write the answers on the board or overhead transparency so students can have the correct answers for study purposes. **Note:** It is a good practice in public speaking and leadership skills for individual students to take charge of leading the discussions of the study questions. Perhaps a different student could go to the front of the class and lead the discussion each day that the study questions are discussed during this unit. Of course, the teacher should guide the discussion when appropriate and be sure to fill in any gaps the students leave.

Activity #2
Distribute the non-fiction reading assignment. Break your class into at least six groups and have students divide the assignment amongst themselves. Each student will also complete a non-fiction reading assignment sheet based on his/her particular topic. The class will be visiting the library media center during Lesson 3 for researching this assignment.

Activity #3
Give students about 15 minutes to preview the study questions and do the vocabulary work for chapters 3-4.

Activity #4
Have students read chapters 3-4 of *Dracula* out loud in class. If time runs out in class, students should do this assignment as homework and have it completed prior to the next class period.

Continue with the oral reading evaluations until all students have be evaluated.

ORAL READING EVALUATION *Dracula*

Name _____ Class____ Date _____

SKILL	EXCELLENT	GOOD	AVERAGE	FAIR	POOR
Fluency	5	4	3	2	1
Clarity	5	4	3	2	1
Audibility	5	4	3	2	1
Pronunciation	5	4	3	2	1
_____	5	4	3	2	1
_____	5	4	3	2	1

Total _____   Grade _____

Comments:

NON-FICTION READING ASSIGNMENT
19th Century Concepts and Ideas

Your group will be presenting to the class a lesson on one of the following:
- the Development of Psychoanalysis
- gender roles in Victorian Society
- class expectations in Victorian Society
- the Industrial Revolution
  - changes in industry
  - changes in medicine/science
- Superstition
- Evolution vs. Creationism

Library Media Center Research:

Using materials from the library and from the Internet (if available), find information supporting your group's topic. Your group will be creating a ten minute mini-lesson on your topic which must include:
- a definition and full explanation of the concept/idea including key people involved
- evidence that Bram Stoker and other authors were affected by the idea(s)
- evidence from the novel *Dracula* supporting the concept/idea
- a poster/collage depicting what you understand about the concept/idea
- 4 multiple-choice questions and 1 short answer question that would need to be answered in at least five complete sentences which will be used during the class presentation

Be sure that:
- each member of the group contributes during the preparation of your lesson
- each member of the group contributes during the delivery of your lesson
- questions for the quiz are thoughtful and reflect the important aspects that you believe students should know about your topic

Grading: Each will be graded on a scale of 1-5, with 1 being the lowest; each is worth 20%.
- individual contribution during the preparation time in class
- individual contribution to the group lesson (equal time plus how well you are familiar with what you are teaching; although you may use notes, you may not merely read information from a sheet
- correct information has been provided to your classmates
- information supports how the idea influenced Bram Stoker and other 19th century authors, especially in Stoker's *Dracula*
- all necessary portions of the project have been addressed (includes poster and quiz)

NONFICTION ASSIGNMENT SHEET
(To be completed after reading the required nonfiction article)

Name _____ Date _____

Title of Nonfiction Read _____

Written By _____ Publication Date _____

I. Factual Summary: Write a short summary of the piece you read.

II. Vocabulary
    1. With which vocabulary words in the piece did you encounter some degree of difficulty?

    2. How did you resolve your lack of understanding with these words?

III. Interpretation: What was the main point the author wanted you to get from reading his work?

IV. Criticism
    1. With which points of the piece did you agree or find easy to accept? Why?

    2. With which points of the piece did you disagree or find difficult to believe? Why?

V. Personal Response: What do you think about this piece? OR How does this piece influence your ideas?

LESSON THREE

Objectives
1. To review the main ideas of chapters 3-4
2. To enhance research skills through a visit to the school's library media center
3. To demonstrate reading comprehension skills through completion of a non-fiction worksheet
4. To improve critical analysis and writing skills through creating a lesson plan
5. To improve social/cooperative learning through working in small groups
6. To preview the study guide questions and vocabulary for chapters 5-6
7. To read chapters 5-6

Activity #1
Give students a few minutes to formulate answers for the study guide questions for chapters 3-4, and then discuss the answers to the questions in detail. Write the answers on the board or overhead transparency so students can have the correct answers for study purposes.

Activity #2
Visit library media center. Students will work in their groups to research their selected 19th century topic and create a mini-lesson to teach. Students will use their sources to complete the non-fiction assignment worksheet.

Activity #3
Tell students to preview the study guide questions and do the vocabulary worksheet for chapters 5-6 and then read those chapters prior to the next class meeting.

LESSON FOUR

Objectives
1. To review the main events and ideas in chapters 5-6
2. To demonstrate reading comprehension by taking a quiz
3. To recognize gothic elements found in tales by the Brothers Grimm
4. To compare and contrast the "Grimm" tales and familiar Disney versions
5. To work in cooperative groups for collaborative learning
6. To preview the study guide questions and vocabulary for chapters 7-8
7. To read chapters 7-8

Activity #1
Give students a few minutes to formulate answers for the study guide questions for chapters 5-6, and then discuss the answers to the questions in detail. Write the answers on the board or overhead transparency so students can have the correct answers for study purposes.

Activity #2
Quiz Chapters 1-6: Distribute quizzes and give students about 10 minutes to complete them.

Note: The quizzes may either be the short answer study guides or the multiple choice version. Have students exchange papers. Grade the quizzes as a class. Collect the papers for recording the grades. (If you used the multiple choice version as a quiz, take a few minutes to discuss the answers for the short answer version if your students are using the short answer version for their study guides.)

Activity #3
Read a translation of the Grimm's fairy tale "Ashenputen" ("Cinderella") or any other classic fairytale that has been revised and made into a Walt Disney movie. (SUGGESTIONS: Grimms' "Sleeping Beauty," "Snow White," or "The Brave Little Tailor" or Hans Christian Anderson's "The Little Mermaid" or Madame Gabrielle-Suzanne Barbot de Villeneuve's "Beauty and the Beast") All of these tales can be found very easily on the Internet.

Students are to make note of any gothic elements that they notice about the tale they are listening to. Students are also to listen for and note any differences in comparison with the Disney version of the tale they are familiar with.

After reading, discuss student responses and note them in two columns on the front board. In groups of three or four, have students discuss why the modern versions are so different. In each version of the tale, what was the message to the children who heard them? How has that message changed? What do the changes show about the differences in the culture of the original tales and modern American culture? Have groups share their findings with entire class.

Activity #4
Give each group copies of various tales that have been "revised" over the years and have students repeat the process. Each group is to create a poster depicting a scene from the ORIGINAL version of the tale that is very different from the modern version. What lesson was trying to be taught to children through this tale?

SUGGESTIONS FROM GRIMM: "The Frog King," "Rapunzel," "Hansel and Grethel," Little Red-Cap," and "Rumplestiltskin." Most students should be familiar with these tales from their childhood.

Activity #5
Tell students to preview the study guide questions and do the vocabulary worksheet for chapters 7-8 and then read those chapters prior to the next class meeting.

LESSON FIVE

Objectives
1. To review the main events and ideas in chapters 7-8
2. To demonstrate an understanding of Stoker's use of imagery through visualization and illustration
3. To increase public speaking skills through sharing information
4. To preview the study guide questions and vocabulary for chapters 9-10
5. To read chapters 9-10

Activity #1

Give students a few minutes to formulate answers for the study guide questions for chapters 7-8, and then discuss the answers to the questions in detail. Write the answers on the board or overhead transparency so students can have the correct answers for study purposes

Activity #2

Have students close their eyes. Read aloud a selected passage from *Dracula* that is an example of vivid imagery. (For example, Signet Classic page 38 "Two were dark . . ." in chapter 3) After reading, have students write down specific images that came into their minds while listening. Discuss how Stoker was able to create that mental picture through the use of words.

Divide class into eight groups and assign each group a chapter from the novel (through chapter 8). Have students read through their assigned chapters to select examples of Stoker's use of imagery. Each group is to discuss Stoker's technique/diction, and then have them select two examples to illustrate. They must also provide a caption for the drawing and indicate the page number.

Activity #3

After the groups are finished with their drawings, they will read the passages orally to the class while classmates close their eyes and listen, making note of images that come to mind. Have some students share what they "saw" in their imaginations. Then have the members of the group share the illustration for the passage and tell how Stoker's words influenced the drawing. Allow any student who claims to have "seen" the image differently to share his/her ideas and defend them with Stoker's words. Repeat for all groups. Display the drawings on the bulletin board.

Activity #4

Tell students to preview the study guide questions and do the vocabulary worksheet for chapters 9-10 and then read those chapters prior to the next class meeting.

LESSON SIX

Objectives
1. To review the main events and ideas in chapters 9-10
2. To widen the breadth of students' knowledge about the topics discussed or touched upon in *Dracula*
3. To check students' nonfiction reading assignments
4. To share collective findings about a particular topic related the 19th century
5. To improve public speaking skills through an oral presentation
6. To preview the study guide questions and vocabulary for chapters 11-12
7. To read chapters 11-12

Activity #1
   Give students a few minutes to formulate answers for the study guide questions for chapters 9-10, and then discuss the answers to the questions in detail. Write the answers on the board or overhead transparency so students can have the correct answers for study purposes

Activity #2
   Ask each group of students to share its prepared oral report about the general topic and about the nonfiction articles read for the unit project assignment. A group presentation evaluation sheet is provided .

   Start with one group's report. Each group member must contribute equally to the presentation. They must share each of the following:
   - a definition and full explanation of the concept/idea including key people involved
   - evidence that Bram Stoker and other authors were affected by the idea(s)
   - evidence from the novel *Dracula* supporting the concept/idea
   - a poster/collage depicting what you understand about the concept/idea

   At the end of the presentation, someone from the group will ask the class the 4 multiple-choice questions that they created and the students who have been listening to the presentation will provide the answers. The group will also write its short answer question that they created on the front board and students at their seats must write a response in at least five complete sentences—these will be collected and assessed by the teacher.

   Repeat with the remaining groups.

   The teacher should collect the non-fiction reading assignment sheets for assessment.

Activity #3
   Tell students to preview the study guide questions and do the vocabulary worksheet for chapters 11-12 and then read those chapters prior to the next class meeting.

GROUP PRESENTATION EVALUATION SHEET
Dracula

Each of the following will be graded on a scale of 1-5, with 1 being the lowest; each is worth 20% of the overall grade.

- **Part I:** Individual contribution during the preparation time in class (This was monitored during media center visit)
- **Part II:** Individual contribution to the group lesson (equal time plus how well he/she is familiar with what he/she is teaching; although students may use notes, they should not merely read information from a sheet, but have it somewhat memorized)
- **Part III:** Individual provided correct information to classmates
- **Part IV:** Information supports how the idea influenced Bram Stoker and other 19th century authors, especially in Stoker's *Dracula*
- **Part V:** Individual has provided all of his/her necessary portion of the group project (including the poster and quiz)

Group Topic: _____

Student Name	Part I	Part II	Part III	Part IV	Part V	Total Score

LESSON SEVEN

Objectives
1. To review the main events and ideas in chapters 11-12
2. To demonstrate reading comprehension by taking a quiz
3. To demonstrate an understanding of characterization through the creation of character posters
4. To demonstrate their understanding of the difference between a physical characteristic and a character trait
5. To practice speaking in front of a group through presentation of the posters
6. To practice note taking skills while listening to others' presentations
7. To preview the study guide questions and vocabulary for chapters 13-14
8. To read chapters 13-14

Activity #1
Give students a few minutes to formulate answers for the study guide questions for chapters 11-12, and then discuss the answers to the questions in detail. Write the answers on the board or overhead transparency so students can have the correct answers for study purposes

Activity #2
Quiz chapters 7-12: Distribute quizzes and give students about 10 minutes to complete them. Have students exchange papers. Grade the quizzes as a class. Collect for recording the grades.

Activity #3
Divide students into 10 pairs/groups for the following: Jonathan Harker, Dracula, Mina Harker, Lucy Westenra, Arthur Holmwood, Renfield, Dr. John Seward, Dr. Van Helsing, Quincey Morris, and the Weird Sisters (vampire women).

Each pair/group will be given a large sheet of construction paper to be used to create a character poster. On each poster, the groups must provide the following:
- the name of the character
- a labeled picture of the character based on the physical description given in the text (labels should contain page numbers as evidence)
- a list of at least three positive character traits with supporting evidence and corresponding page numbers for each
- a list of at least three negative character traits with supporting evidence and corresponding page numbers for each

NOTE: Encourage the students to try to find SOME redeeming quality for Count Dracula (ie. intelligence, excellent planner) and the Weird Sisters.

Activity #4
After students finish their posters, each pair/group must get up in front of the class and share the information about its particular character. Those who are not presenting must take notes about the other characters. Remind students that they will all be responsible for being able to identify all of the characters on the unit test.

Activity #5
> Tell students to preview the study guide questions and do the vocabulary worksheet for chapters 13-14 and then read those chapters prior to the next class meeting.

LESSON EIGHT

Objectives
1. To review the main events and ideas from chapters 13-14
2. To demonstrate knowledge of various types of conflict by examining Bram Stoker's *Dracula*
3. To practice public speaking
4. To preview the study guide questions and vocabulary for chapters 15-17
5. To read chapters 15-17

Activity #1
    Give students a few minutes to formulate answers for the study guide questions for chapters 13-14, and then discuss the answers to the questions in detail. Write the answers on the board or overhead transparency so students can have the correct answers for study purposes.

Activity #2
    Ask students to identify the various types of conflicts found in literature (man vs. man, man vs. society, man vs. nature, man vs. the unknown, or man vs. self). NOTE: The term "man" is used as referring to a member of the race of "mankind." Create a chart on the front board with each type of a conflict as a heading. Have students provide examples from literature, movies, television, or life of each type of conflict, and ask them to fill their responses in on the board. Try to come up with at least five for each type.

Activity #3
    Divide the class into seven groups and assign each group one of the following: Ch. 1-2, Ch. 3-4, Ch. 5-6, Ch. 7-8, Ch. 9-10, Ch. 11-12, or Ch. 13-14 from Bram Stoker's *Dracula*.
    Each group is to identify as many conflicts as possible for its assigned chapters and try to identify each conflict's TYPE. Ask them to try to find at least two examples of each TYPE of conflict. Students must also list at least three elements of gothic literature that they find in their assigned chapters (see list of gothic elements from introductory lesson).
    Each group (go in order of the chapters) will share its findings and the rest of the students will take notes on what they hear. Everyone will end up with a list of conflicts for the first fourteen chapters of *Dracula*.

Activity #4
    Tell students to preview the study guide questions and do the vocabulary worksheet for chapters 15-17 and then read those chapters prior to the next class meeting.

LESSON NINE

Objectives
1. To review the main events and ideas from chapters 15-17
2. To increase research skills by using the library media center
3. To further explore the gothic genre
4. To practice writing to inform
5. To preview the study guide questions and vocabulary for chapters 18-19
6. To read chapters 18-19

Activity #1
   Give students a few minutes to formulate answers for the study guide questions for chapters 15-17, and then discuss the answers to the questions in detail. Write the answers on the board or overhead transparency so students can have the correct answers for study purposes

Activity #2
   Distribute Writing Assignment #1 and discuss the directions in detail.

Activity #3
   Take students to the library media center where you (or the librarian) will have already selected books of short stories by various authors who wrote in the gothic genre.
Students are to:
   - select an author from the proposed list (see below)
   - find two short stories written by that author for use in the assignment (NOTE: no two students may select the same story).
   - For those with internet connections, students may download and print out many of the stories that fit this assignment. Complete short stories may be downloaded at:
     - Classic Short Stories   http://www.bnl.com/shorts/
     - Classic Reader   http://www.classicreader.com/toc.php/sid.6/
   - Once students have made their selections, they may begin reading the stories and taking notes for the writing assignment.

Authors Who Wrote/Write in the Gothic Genre:
   - Edgar Allan Poe
   - Ambrose Bierce
   - Nathaniel Hawthorne
   - H. P. Lovecraft
   - Stephen King
   - Ann Lemoine
   - H. G. Wells
   - Robert Louis Stevenson
   - Sir Arthur Conan Doyle
   - Oscar Wilde
   - W. W. Jacobs
   - Saki (h. H. Munro)
   - Anne Rice
   - Edith Wharton

Activity #4
   Tell students to preview the study guide questions and do the vocabulary worksheet for chapters 18-19 and then read those chapters prior to the next class meeting.

WRITING ASSIGNMENT #1-*Dracula*
Writing for Information

PROMPT
You are reading the gothic novel *Dracula* by Bram Stoker, and the class has been exploring Stoker's use of specific gothic elements in his novel. You will choose an author from a select list of authors in the gothic genre and find two short stories written by that author. The teacher will poll the class to see that no two students are writing about the same short story (although they may use the same author). You must also find biographical information about the author.

PREWRITING
After reading the short stories, make a list of 'gothic' elements that the author used. Be sure to keep a list of specific evidence from the text that supports the author's use of a particular element. Write an essay in which you provide biographical information about the author and in which you discuss the author's use of specific gothic elements in the stories you selected. You must support your ideas with textual quotations from the stories as well as evidence you collect from secondary sources (biographical information).

DRAFTING
Introduce your topic in the first paragraph, being sure to end with a thesis statement. Be sure to include the titles and author of the stories that you will be analyzing. Then write seven body paragraphs (one for biographical information, and three paragraphs for **each** of the two stories), each describing how the author uses specific gothic elements in his/her writing. Be sure to include embedded quotations from your biographical research and from both stories in your body paragraphs as support for your thesis. Also, incorporate at least three vocabulary words from the unit into your essay. Finally, conclude by attempting to formulate a hypothesis about why people seem to enjoy being scared. End the conclusion by challenging your reader in some way.

PEER CONFERENCE/REVISING
When you finish the draft, ask another student to look at it. You may want to give the student your worksheets and articles so he/she can double check to see you have included all the information you intended to include. After reading, he/she should tell you what is best about your essay, which parts were difficult to understand or follow, and ways in which your essay could be improved. Reread your essay considering your critic's comments and make the corrections you think are necessary.

PROOFREADING/EDITING
Do a final proofreading of your essay, double-checking your grammar, spelling, organization, and the clarity of your ideas.

PREPARE CLASS PRESENTATION
Make a poster depicting the life of the author, his/her link to the gothic genre, and the specific atmosphere the author tried to create. Include references to the stories you worked with. In a 7-10 minute presentation, share your findings with your classmates.

WRITING EVALUATION FORM - *Dracula*

Name _____ Date _____

Grade _____

Circle One For Each Item:

Grammar: correct errors noted on paper

Spelling: correct errors noted on paper

Punctuation: correct errors noted on paper

Legibility: excellent   good   fair   poor

_____   excellent   good   fair   poor

_____   excellent   good   fair   poor

Strengths:

Weaknesses:

Comments/Suggestions:

LESSON TEN

Objectives
1. To review the main events and ideas from chapters 18-19
2. To demonstrate reading comprehension by taking a quiz
3. To preview the study guide questions and vocabulary for chapters 20-21
4. To read chapters 20-21

Activity #1

Give students a few minutes to formulate answers for the study guide questions for chapters 18-19, and then discuss the answers to the questions in detail. Write the answers on the board or overhead transparency so students can have the correct answers for study purposes.

Activity #2

Quiz chapters 13-17: Distribute quizzes and give students about 10 minutes to complete them. Have students exchange papers. Grade the quizzes as a class. Collect for recording the grades.

Activity #3

Give students 15 minutes to review the study guide questions and do vocabulary work for chapters 20-21. Students should read chapters 20-21 prior to the next class meeting. If time remains in class, students may begin working on this assignment.

LESSON ELEVEN

Objectives
1. To review the main events and ideas from chapters 20-21
2. To create poetic epitaphs for one another
3. To preview the study guide questions and vocabulary for chapters 22-23
4. To read chapters 22-23

Activity #1
Give students a few minutes to formulate answers for the study guide questions for chapters 20-21, and then discuss the answers to the questions in detail. Write the answers on the board or overhead transparency so students can have the correct answers for study purposes

Activity #2
Put students in pairs. Have each student interview his/her partner in order to learn more about him/her and write the responses down on paper. Students should ask such questions as:
What do you like to do for fun?
What do you hope to be when you grow up?
Where do you hope to live as an adult? (city, country, etc.)
What kind of person do you want to be? (name at least three specific traits)
What three things would you like people to remember about you in the future?

After interviewing each other, remind students about the scene in Bram Stoker's *Dracula* in which Mina and Lucy met an old man in the cemetery. Recall the discussion about the epitaphs and how the old man complained that the tombstones "lied". Students will use the interview responses to create a true poetic epitaph (at least ten lines that have some sort of a rhyme scheme) that could be engraved on this person's tombstone. Draw the tombstone and write the poem on it.

Tombstones may be displayed on a bulletin board.

Activity #3
Tell students to preview the study guide questions and do the vocabulary worksheet for chapters 22-23 and then read those chapters prior to the next class meeting.

LESSON TWELVE

Objectives
1. To review the main ideas and events in chapters 22-23
2. To demonstrate reading comprehension by taking a quiz
3. To work independently on the research assignment
4. To preview the study guide questions and vocabulary for chapters 24-25
5. To read chapters 24-25

Activity #1
   Give students a few minutes to formulate answers for the study guide questions for chapters 22 and 23, and then discuss the answers to the questions in detail. Write the answers on the board or overhead transparency so students can have the correct answers for study purposes.

Activity #2
   Quiz chapters 18-21: Distribute quizzes and give students about 10 minutes to complete them. Have students exchange papers. Grade the quizzes as a class. Collect for recording the grades.

Activity #3
   Allow students to use sources they gathered from the library media center to work independently on research assignments. This will give students an opportunity to ask questions about the assignment if necessary.

Activity #4
   Tell students to preview the study guide questions and do the vocabulary worksheet for chapters 24-25 and then read those chapters prior to the next class meeting.

LESSON THIRTEEN

Objectives
1. To review the main events and ideas in chapters 24-25
2. To demonstrate knowledge of various types of conflicts and Gothic elements in chapters 15-25
3. To preview the study guide questions and vocabulary for chapters 26-27
4. To read chapters 26-27

Activity #1

Give students a few minutes to formulate answers for the study guide questions for chapters 24-25, and then discuss the answers to the questions in detail. Write the answers on the board or overhead transparency so students can have the correct answers for study purposes.

Activity #2

Divide the class into five groups and assign each group one of the following: Ch. 15-17, Ch. 18-19, Ch. 20-21, Ch. 22-23, or Ch.24-25 from Bram Stoker's *Dracula*.

Using their study guides, each group is to identify as many conflicts as possible for its assigned chapters and try to identify each conflict's TYPE. Ask them to try to find at least two examples of each TYPE of conflict. Students must also list at least three elements of gothic literature that they find in their assigned chapters (see list of gothic elements from introductory lesson).

Each group (go in order of the chapters) will share its findings and the rest of the students will take notes on what they hear. Everyone will end up with a list of conflicts for chapters 15-25 of *Dracula*.

Activity #3

Give students a few minutes to preview the study guide questions and do the vocabulary worksheet for chapters 24-25.

Activity #3

Have students read Chapters 26-27 of *Dracula* silently for the remainder of the class time. This assignment should be completed prior to the next class meeting.

LESSON FOURTEEN

Objectives
1. To review the main events and ideas from chapters 26-27
2. To demonstrate reading comprehension by taking a quiz
3. To give students the opportunity to practice creative writing
4. To demonstrate the ability to create a specific "voice" for a character through journal writing
5. To demonstrate their understanding of a character's point of view through journal writing

Activity #1

Give students a few minutes to formulate answers for the study guide questions for chapters 26-27, and then discuss the answers to the questions in detail. Write the answers on the board or overhead transparency so students can have the correct answers for study purposes

Activity #2

Quiz chapters 22-27: Distribute quizzes and give students about 10 minutes to complete them. Have students exchange papers. Grade the quizzes as a class. Collect for recording the grades.

Activity #3

Distribute Writing Assignment #2: Creative Writing. Students will create a journal for a character whose point of view is rarely (if ever) expressed in Bram Stoker's *Dracula*. Give students the remainder of the class period to work on their journals, and tell them when journals are due for grading.

WRITING ASSIGNMENT #2 - *Dracula*
Creative Writing

PROMPT:
Bram Stoker's novel is written in the form of an epistolary (a series of letters and journal entries). The reader is primarily invited into the private thoughts of Jonathan Harker, Mina Harker, Lucy Westenra, Professor Van Helsing, and Dr. John Seward. However, there are some characters whose point of view the reader does not have the privilege of hearing. How might the reader's opinion of these characters change if he/she had been allowed to know their private thoughts as well? Your assignment is to select one of the following characters and create a journal that contains at least five fifty-word entries.

PREWRITING:
Choose one of these characters:

Renfield	Count Dracula	Arthur Holmwood
Quincey Morris	Mrs. Westenra	one of the female vampires

Go through the book and on a piece of paper jot down the page numbers of the scenes of which your character is involved. Review the scenes and make notes about what you think his/her point of view of the event would be.

DRAFTING:
Remember that there were no word processors in the 1800's, and that most diaries were written by hand. Not everyone had a typewriter like Mina or a phonograph like Dr. Seward! Be sure to create an appropriate voice for the character based on his/her actions and not merely other characters' opinions. Since this is a PROJECT, make the booklet look like an old journal from the 1800's, and remember to date your entries. While attempting to emulate Stoker's formal writing style (this IS Victorian England!), you are required to correctly use three vocabulary words from the unit per journal entry. Write one journal entry for each of the five scenes you have chosen.

PROMPT
    When you finish the rough draft of your journal, ask a student who sits near you to read it. After reading your rough draft, he/she should tell you what he/she liked best about your work, which parts were difficult to understand, and ways in which your work could be improved. Reread your journal considering your critic's comments, and make the corrections you think are necessary.

PROOFREADING
    Do a final proofreading of your journal double-checking your grammar, spelling, organization, and the clarity of your ideas.

WRITING EVALUATION FORM - *Dracula*

Name _____ Date _____

Grade _____

Circle One For Each Item:

Grammar: correct errors noted on paper

Spelling: correct errors noted on paper

Punctuation: correct errors noted on paper

Legibility: excellent   good   fair   poor

_____   excellent   good   fair   poor

_____   excellent   good   fair   poor

Strengths:

Weaknesses:

Comments/Suggestions:

LESSON FIFTEEN

Objectives
1. To read and identify Gothic elements of poetry
2. To illustrate gothic images from poetry and use citations from the poem as captions

Activity #1

Distribute and read aloud Edgar Allan Poe's "Annabelle Lee." Students follow along while underlining specific passages that seem to have a gothic "feel" to them. Create three columns on the front board (Plot, Imagery, Other Figurative Language) and have students make note of at least two examples where Poe's use of these devices lent a gothic air to the poem. Students share responses and write them under the appropriate categories on the front board.

Activity #2

Divide class into four groups and give each group copies of one of these four poems:
"The Grave" by Robert Blair
"The Fatal Sisters" by Thomas Gray
"Elegy Written in a Country Churchyard" by Thomas Gray
"The Conqueror Worm" by Edgar Allan Poe
You may also choose other poems instead.

NOTE: The poems are included in their entirety in this unit plan; they have gone into public domain.

Students will repeat the exercise done as a large group within their small groups. They will read the poem assigned to their group, underlining it for its gothic elements. They will create a chart that lists at least three examples (with cited line numbers) of each: plot, imagery, and other figurative language.

Students will EACH illustrate a DIFFERENT image from the poem and copy the line from the poem onto their drawing as a caption.

Groups will share findings by providing a BRIEF plot summary of the poem for their classmates, point out the gothic elements from the group's chart, and each person will share his/her illustration and explain how it supports the poet's use of gothic elements in the poem.

Illustrations may be displayed on a bulletin board.

You may need additional class time to complete this activity.

"Annabel Lee" by Edgar Allan Poe

It was many and many a year ago,
 In a kingdom by the sea,
That a maiden there lived whom you may know
 By the name of Annabel Lee;--
And this maiden she lived with no other thought
Than to love and be loved by me.

I was a child and *she* was a child,
 In this kingdom by the sea;
But we loved with a love that was more than love--
 I and my Annabel Lee--
With a love that the wingéd seraphs in Heaven
 Coveted her and me.

And this was the reason that, long ago,
 In this kingdom by the sea,
A wind blew out of a cloud, chilling
 My beautiful Annabel Lee;
So that her high-born kinsmen came
 And bore her away from me,
To shut her up in a sepulchre,
 In this kingdom by the sea.

The angels, not half so happy in Heaven,
 Went envying her and me--
Yes!--that was the reason (as all men know,
 In this kingdom by the sea)
That the wind came out of the cloud by night,
 Chilling and killing my Annabel Lee.

But our love it was stronger by far than the love
 Of those who were older than we--
 Of many far wiser than we--
And neither the angels in Heaven above,
 Nor the demons down under the sea,
Can ever dissever my soul from the soul
 Of the beautiful Annabel Lee:--

For the moon never beams, without bringing me dreams
 Of the beautiful Annabel Lee;
And the stars never rise, but I feel the bright eyes
 Of the beautiful Annabel Lee:--
And so, all the night-tide, I lie down by the side
Of my darling--my darling--my life and my bride,
 In her sepulchre there by the sea--
 In her tomb by the sounding sea.

"The Grave" by Robert Blair

(an excerpt)

While some affect the sun, and some the shade.
Some flee the city, some the hermitage;
Their aims as various, as the roads they take
In journeying thro' life;--the task be mine,
To paint the gloomy horrors of the tomb;
Th' appointed place of rendezvous, where all
These travellers meet.--Thy succours I implore,
Eternal King! whose potent arm sustains
The keys of Hell and Death.--The Grave, dread thing!
Men shiver when thou'rt named: Nature appall'd
Shakes off her wonted firmness.--Ah ! how dark
The long-extended realms, and rueful wastes!
Where nought but silence reigns, and night, dark night,
Dark as was chaos, ere the infant Sun
Was roll'd together, or had tried his beams
Athwart the gloom profound.--The sickly taper,
By glimm'ring thro' thy low-brow'd misty vaults,
(Furr'd round with mouldy damps, and ropy slime)
Lets fall a supernumerary horror,
And only serves to make thy night more irksome.
Well do I know thee by thy trusty yew,
Cheerless, unsocial plant! that loves to dwell
'Midst skulls and coffins, epitaphs and worms:
Where light-heel'd ghosts, and visionary shades,
Beneath the wan, cold moon (as fame reports)
Embodied thick, perform their mystic rounds,
No other merriment, dull tree! is thine.

See yonder hallow'd fane;--the pious work
Of names once fam'd, now dubious or forgot,
And buried midst the wreck of things which were;
There lie interr'd the more illustrious dead.
The wind is up:--hark! how it howls!--Methinks,
'Till now, I never heard a sound so dreary:
Doors creak, and windows clap, and night's foul bird,
Rook'd in the spire, screams loud; the gloomy aisles
Black plaster'd, and hung round with shreds of 'scutcheons,
And tatter'd coats of arms, send back the sound,
Laden with heavier airs, from the low vaults,
The mansions of the dead.--Rous'd from their slumbers,
In grim array the grisly spectres rise,
Grin horrible, and, obstinately sullen,
Pass and repass, hush'd as the foot of night.
Again the screech-owl shrieks--ungracious sound!
I'll hear no more; it makes one's blood run chill.

   Quite round the pile, a row of reverend elms,
(Coeval near with that) all ragged show,
Long lash'd by the rude winds. Some rift half down
Their branchless trunks; others so thin at top,
That scarce two crows can lodge in the same tree.
Strange things, the neighbours say, have happen'd here;
Wild shrieks have issued from the hollow tombs;
Dead men have come again, and walk'd about;
And the great bell has toll'd, unrung, untouch'd.
(Such tales their cheer at wake or gossipping,
When it draws near to witching time of night.)

   Oft in the lone church yard at night I've seen,
By glimpse of moonshine chequering thro' the trees,
The school boy, with his satchel in his hand,
Whistling aloud to bear his courage up,
And lightly tripping o'er the long flat stones,
(With nettles skirted, and with moss o'ergrown,)
That tell in homely phrase who lie below.
Sudden he starts, and hears, or thinks he hears,
The sound of something purring at his heels;
Full fast he flies, and dare not look behind him,
'Till, out of breath, he overtakes his fellows,
Who gather round and wonder at the tale
Of horrid apparition tall and ghastly,
That walks at dead of night, or takes his stand
O'er some new-open'd grave; and (strange to tell!)
Evanishes at crowing of the cock.

   The new-made widow, too, I've sometimes 'spy'd,
Sad sight! slow moving o'er the prostrate dead:
Listless, she crawls along in doleful black,
While bursts of sorrow gush from either eye,
Fast falling down her now untasted cheek,
Prone on the lowly grave of the dear man
She drops; while busy meddling memory,
In barbarous succession, musters up
The past endearments of their softer hours,
 Tenacious of its theme. Still, still she thinks
 She sees him, and indulging the fond thought,
 Clings yet more closely to the senseless turf,
 Nor heeds the passenger who looks that way.

"The Fatal Sisters": An Ode by Thomas Gray

(FROM THE NORSE TONGUE)

Now the storm begins to lower,
(Haste, the loom of Hell prepare.)
Iron-sleet of arrowy shower
Hurtles in the darken'd air.

Glitt'ring lances are the loom,
Where the dusky warp we strain,
Weaving many a soldier's doom,
Orkney's woe, and Randver's bane.

See the grisly texture grow,
('Tis of human entrails made,)
And the weights, that play below,
Each a gasping warrior's head.

Shafts for shuttles, dipt in gore,
Shoot the trembling cords along.
Sword, that once a monarch bore,
Keep the tissue close and strong.

Mista black, terrific maid,
Sangrida, and Hilda see,
Join the wayward work to aid:
Tis the woof of victory.

Ere the ruddy sun be set,
Pikes must shiver, javelins sing,
Blade with clatt'ring buckler meet,
Hauberk crash, and helmet ring.

(Weave the crimson web of war)
Let us go, and let us fly,
Where our friends the conflict share,
Where they triumph, where they die.

As the paths of fate we tread,
Wading thro' th' ensanguin'd field:
Gondula, and Geira, spread
O'er the youthful king your shield.

We the reins to slaughter give,
Ours to kill, and ours to spare:
Spite of danger he shall live.
(Weave the crimson web of war.)

They, whom once the desert-beach
Pent within its bleak domain,
Soon their ample sway shall stretch
O'er the plenty of the plain.

Low the dauntless earl is laid
Gor'd with many a gaping wound:
Fate demands a nobler head;
Soon a king shall bite the ground.

Long his loss shall Erin weep,
Ne'er again his likeness see;
Long her strains in sorrow steep,
Strains of immortality.

Horror covers all the heath,
Clouds of carnage blot the sun.
Sisters, weave the web of death;
Sisters, cease, the work is done.

Hail the task, and hail the hands!
Songs of joy and triumph sing!
Joy to the victorious bands;
Triumph to the younger king.

Mortal, thou that hear'st the tale,
Learn the tenor of our song.
Scotland thro' each winding vale
Far and wide the notes prolong.

Sisters, hence with spurs of speed:
 Each her thund'ring falchion wield;
Each bestride her sable steed.
Hurry, hurry to the field.

"Elegy Written in a Country Churchyard" by Thomas Gray
(an excerpt)

The curfew tolls the knell of parting day,
      The lowing herd wind slowly o'er the lea,
The plowman homeward plods his weary way,
      And leaves the world to darkness and to me.

Now fades the glimm'ring landscape on the sight,
      And all the air a solemn stillness holds,
Save where the beetle wheels his droning flight,
      And drowsy tinklings lull the distant folds;

Save that from yonder ivy-mantled tow'r
      The moping owl does to the moon complain
Of such, as wand'ring near her secret bow'r,
      Molest her ancient solitary reign.

Beneath those rugged elms, that yew-tree's shade,
      Where heaves the turf in many a mould'ring heap,
Each in his narrow cell for ever laid,
      The rude forefathers of the hamlet sleep.

The breezy call of incense-breathing Morn,
      The swallow twitt'ring from the straw-built shed,
The cock's shrill clarion, or the echoing horn,
      No more shall rouse them from their lowly bed.

For them no more the blazing hearth shall burn,
      Or busy housewife ply her evening care:
No children run to lisp their sire's return,
      Or climb his knees the envied kiss to share.

Oft did the harvest to their sickle yield,
      Their furrow oft the stubborn glebe has broke;
How jocund did they drive their team afield!
      How bow'd the woods beneath their sturdy stroke!

Let not Ambition mock their useful toil,
      Their homely joys, and destiny obscure;
Nor Grandeur hear with a disdainful smile
      The short and simple annals of the poor.

The boast of heraldry, the pomp of pow'r,
      And all that beauty, all that wealth e'er gave,
Awaits alike th' inevitable hour.
      The paths of glory lead but to the grave.

Nor you, ye proud, impute to these the fault,
      If Mem'ry o'er their tomb no trophies raise,
Where thro' the long-drawn aisle and fretted vault
      The pealing anthem swells the note of praise.

Can storied urn or animated bust
      Back to its mansion call the fleeting breath?
Can Honour's voice provoke the silent dust,
      Or Flatt'ry soothe the dull cold ear of Death?

Perhaps in this neglected spot is laid
      Some heart once pregnant with celestial fire;
Hands, that the rod of empire might have sway'd,
      Or wak'd to ecstasy the living lyre.

But Knowledge to their eyes her ample page
      Rich with the spoils of time did ne'er unroll;
Chill Penury repress'd their noble rage,
      And froze the genial current of the soul.

Full many a gem of purest ray serene,
      The dark unfathom'd caves of ocean bear:
Full many a flow'r is born to blush unseen,
      And waste its sweetness on the desert air.

Some village-Hampden, that with dauntless breast
      The little tyrant of his fields withstood;
Some mute inglorious Milton here may rest,
      Some Cromwell guiltless of his country's blood.

Th' applause of list'ning senates to command,
      The threats of pain and ruin to despise,
To scatter plenty o'er a smiling land,
      And read their hist'ry in a nation's eyes,

Their lot forbade: nor circumscrib'd alone
      Their growing virtues, but their crimes confin'd;
Forbade to wade through slaughter to a throne,
      And shut the gates of mercy on mankind,

The struggling pangs of conscious truth to hide,
      To quench the blushes of ingenuous shame,
Or heap the shrine of Luxury and Pride
      With incense kindled at the Muse's flame.

Far from the madding crowd's ignoble strife,
      Their sober wishes never learn'd to stray;
Along the cool sequester'd vale of life
      They kept the noiseless tenor of their way.

"The Conqueror Worm" by Edgar Allan Poe

Lo! 'tis a gala night
   Within the lonesome latter years!
An angel throng, bewinged, bedight
   In veils, and drowned in tears,
Sit in a theatre, to see
   A play of hopes and fears,
While the orchestra breathes fitfully
   The music of the spheres.

Mimes, in the form of God on high,
   Mutter and mumble low,
And hither and thither fly-
   Mere puppets they, who come and go
At bidding of vast formless things
   That shift the scenery to and fro,
Flapping from out their Condor wings
   Invisible Woe!

That motley drama- oh, be sure
   It shall not be forgot!
With its Phantom chased for evermore,
   By a crowd that seize it not,
Through a circle that ever returneth in
   To the self-same spot,
And much of Madness, and more of Sin,
   And Horror the soul of the plot.

But see, amid the mimic rout
   A crawling shape intrude!
A blood-red thing that writhes from out
   The scenic solitude!
It writhes!- it writhes!- with mortal pangs
   The mimes become its food,
And seraphs sob at vermin fangs
   In human gore imbued.

Out- out are the lights- out all!
   And, over each quivering form,
The curtain, a funeral pall,
   Comes down with the rush of a storm,
While the angels, all pallid and wan,
   Uprising, unveiling, affirm
That the play is the tragedy, "Man,"
   And its hero the Conqueror Worm.

LESSON SIXTEEN

Objective
    To review all of the vocabulary work done in this unit

Activity
    Choose one (or more) of the vocabulary review activities listed below and spend your class period as directed in the activity. Some of the materials for these review activities are located in the Vocabulary Resource Materials section in this LitPlan.

VOCABULARY REVIEW ACTIVITIES

1. Divide your class into two teams and have an old-fashioned spelling or definition bee.

2. Give each of your students (or students in groups of two, three or four) a *Dracula* Vocabulary Word Search Puzzle. The person (group) to find all of the vocabulary words in the puzzle first wins.

3. Give students a *Dracula* Vocabulary Word Search Puzzle without the word list. The person or group to find the most vocabulary words in the puzzle wins.

4. Use a *Dracula* Vocabulary Crossword Puzzle. Put the puzzle onto a transparency on the overhead projector (so everyone can see it), and do the puzzle together as a class.

5. Give students a *Dracula* Vocabulary Matching Worksheet to do.

6. Divide your class into two teams. Use *Dracula* vocabulary words with their letters jumbled as a word list. Student 1 from Team A faces off against Student 1 from Team B. You write the first jumbled word on the board. The first student (1A or 1B) to unscramble the word wins the chance for his/her team to score points. If 1A wins the jumble, go to student 2A and give him/her a definition. He/she must give you the correct spelling of the vocabulary word which fits that definition. If he/she does, Team A scores a point, and you give student 3A a definition for which you expect a correctly spelled matching vocabulary word. Continue giving Team A definitions until some team member makes an incorrect response. An incorrect response sends the game back to the jumbled-word face off, this time with students 2A and 2B. Instead of repeating giving definitions to the first few students of each team, continue with the student after the one who gave the last incorrect response on the team. For example, if Team B wins the jumbled-word face-off, and student 5B gave the last incorrect answer for Team B, you would start this round of definition questions with student 6B, and so on. The team with the most points wins!

7. Have students write a story in which they correctly use as many vocabulary words as possible. Have students read their compositions orally! Post the most original compositions on your bulletin board!

LESSON SEVENTEEN

Objectives
To discuss the novel on a deeper level

Activity
Choose the questions from the Extra Discussion Questions/Writing Assignments which seem most appropriate for your students. A class discussion of these questions is most effective if students have been given the opportunity to formulate answers to the questions prior to the discussion. To this end, you may either have all the students formulate answers to all the questions, divide your class into groups and assign one or more questions to each group, or you could assign one question to each student in your class. The option you choose will make a difference in the amount of class time needed for this activity.

NOTE: The use of graphic organizers may be helpful to students in preparing their answers. Encourage them to use any diagrams or graphics that they feel are necessary.

EXTRA WRITING ASSIGNMENTS/DISCUSSION QUESTIONS - *Dracula*

Interpretation
1. Why do Van Helsing, Dr. Seward, and Quincey Morris vow never to tell Arthur about the fact that they, too, gave blood to Lucy through transfusion?
2. Van Helsing tells Dr. Seward the he must return to Amsterdam to think. What is it he needs to think about? What clues does Bram Stoker give the reader about Van Helsing and his studies?
3. Where is the climax of this novel? Explain your choice.
4. Why does Dracula entice Renfield with the promise of many lives? What does he want from Renfield?
5. Why does Renfield turn against Count Dracula?
6. Discuss three specific character traits for each of the following: Jonathan Harker, Mina Harker, Van Helsing, Count Dracula. Support the traits with evidence from the text.
7. What elements of setting are important to the Gothic novel? How would the novel have been different if it had been set in New York City? A tropical island? How would the setting have to be adjusted in order to maintain a gothic quality?
8. Dracula may be considered an epistolary novel. This means that the plot is revealed through a series of letters and diary entries. What makes this technique more effective as opposed to a third person account? From whose point of view is this novel presented? (There are several.) How would a change of point of view affect the overall novel?

Critical
1. Present the students' questions that they wrote for their 19th century ideas project. Share student responses. Revisit each of the following categories and discuss how each was presented in Bram Stoker's *Dracula*.
    a. The Development of Psychoanalysis
    b. Gender Roles in Victorian Society
    c. Class Expectations in Victorian Society
    d. The Industrial Revolution
    e. Changes in Medicine/Science
    f. Superstition
    g. Evolution vs. Creationism
2. When the vampire Lucy is to be destroyed, why is it significant that Arthur is the one to strike the blow that sets her free? What comments on female sexuality in the Victorian era might Stoker have been making in this scene?
3. How does the gothic setting contribute to the overall mood or atmosphere of the novel? Give examples of how Bram Stoker uses setting to create a specific atmosphere.
4. Note that both Count Dracula and Renfield mention that drinking blood will bring eternal life. Discuss how this could be a twisted parallel to the Christian practice of Holy Communion. Why is it significant that Renfield does not want to be responsible for the souls of the creatures he eats? How does that create a contrast for Count Dracula?
5. Compare and contrast Lucy and Mina.
6. Compare and contrast Jonathan, Quincy, and Arthur.

7. Examine the following themes in *Dracula*. What message does Bram Stoker seem to be sending to his readers about each theme?
    a. good vs. evil
    b. the power of love
    c. the power of fear
    d. the power of compassion

Critical/Personal Response
1. Suppose Mina had been first attacked by the Count and it was Lucy who later filled Mina's role. Based on what you know of each person's character, how might the novel have been different?
2. Suppose Lucy had decided to accept Dr. Seward's proposal of marriage. Would that choice have affected Arthur's or Quincey's roles in her redemption? What if she had chosen Quincey Morris?
3. How might the character of Arthur have been different if Van Helsing, Quincey Morris, and Dr. Seward told him that they, too, had given blood transfusions to Lucy?
4. What if the men had not caught up to the carriage carrying the Count's box to his castle. Suppose a different ending to the novel. Would that have been a satisfactory conclusion?
5. Thinking back over the classroom presentations about short stories in the gothic genre, examine what archetypal characters seem to appear over and over again (such as the Damsel in Distress, the Gallant but Tormented Hero, The Evil Villain/Monster that comes in a variety of forms: vampires, wolfmen, "created" creatures, ghosts, etc.). How did the various authors from the class presentations present these archetypes yet still manage to create a unique story? How did Bram Stoker use these archetypes in *Dracula*?
6. List as many superstitions as you can think of. What role does superstition play? What is the role of superstition in Bram Stoker's *Dracula*? What do various superstitions say about the cultures who preserve them?
7. Note that it is Van Helsing's use of the consecrated Communion wafer that both destroys Dracula's lair and protects him from harm. What might be Bram Stoker's view of religion based on this detail?
8. For each of the following characters, select an object and explain how that object could be used to symbolize that person's particular character traits:
    A. Abraham Van Helsing
    B. Lucy Westenra
    C. Mina Harker
    D. Jonathan Harker
    e. Renfield
    f. Count Dracula
    g. Arthur Holmwood
    h. Quincey Morris

Personal Response
1. Do you enjoy being scared? Why or why not? Explain what parts of *Dracula* scared you and why.
2. What age do you think is most appropriate for reading novels like *Dracula*? Explain why.
3. Do you intend to read more books from the 19th Century Gothic genre? Why or why not?
4. Which of the characters do you identify with the most? Why?
5. Fear is categorized as a negative emotion, yet many people seem to like to be scared. They seek thrill rides at amusement parks, go sky-diving, race cars, and watch horror movies. Those who read gothic literature (especially horror literature) fall into a similar category of those who seem to like to be scared. What possible attraction might all of these activities draw for people?

6. What influence of gothic literature can be found in today's movies? Video games? Could they be truly categorized as "Gothic"? Why or why not?

LESSON EIGHTEEN

Objective
    To work independently on creative projects

Activity #1
    Students will work in class on posters for their Gothic authors research project. Provide paper, crayons/colored pencils, scissors, magazines (for cutting pictures that may support a specific story's theme), and glue/tape. While students are working, play some gothic-sounding music in the background.

Activity #2
    Students may work on their character journals using the supplies listed above.

LESSON NINETEEN

Objective
    To improve critical analysis and writing skill through writing a letter

Activity
    Distribute Writing Assignment #3. Discuss the directions in detail and give students ample time to complete the assignment.

    Students will write an in-class persuasive letter to their local school board as to whether or not Gothic literature should be taught in their school. Students are to bring finished essays to class tomorrow for peer-editing and revising.

    Note: While students are writing, call individual students to your desk or some other private area for a writing conference based on the first two writing assignments in this unit. A teacher evaluation form is included in this unit for your convenience.

WRITING ASSIGNMENT #3 - *Dracula*
Persuasive Writing

PROMPT:
There are many people who are of the opinion that an interest in Gothic or Horror literature is sick and demonic and has no place in the classroom. They believe that this genre merely glorifies society's already violent tendencies and perpetuates the deterioration of moral values. On the other hand, there are those who believe that the Gothic or Horror genre offers much in literary merit and deserves to be included in the educational canon. Its examination of the human psyche helps create pathos among individuals, and its reliance on figurative language expands the imagination. Write a persuasive letter to your Board of Education explaining your position as to whether Gothic/Horror literature like *Dracula* should be taught in your school.

PREWRITING:
Which view do you agree with? Should Gothic/Horror literature like Bram Stoker's *Dracula* continue to be a part of your school curriculum, or should it be removed?

DRAFTING:
Be sure to defend your position with at least three specific excerpts from Bram Stoker's *Dracula*, and offer an explanation of why these excerpts support your opinion.

If taking the "Pro" position, recommend other Gothic literature pieces that could be taught as well. If taking the "Con" stance, cite three specific excepts from Bram Stoker's *Dracula* that you feel are particularly offensive to a classroom environment. Make suggestions for literature you feel would be more classroom appropriate.

Appropriately incorporate the use of at least four vocabulary words from the unit in their letter.

PROOFREADING
   Do a final proofreading of your paper double-checking your grammar, spelling, organization, and the clarity of your ideas.

   NOTE: Bring the final copy of your letter to the next class meeting.

WRITING EVALUATION FORM - *Dracula*

Name _____ Date _____

Grade _____

Circle One For Each Item:

Grammar: correct errors noted on paper

Spelling: correct errors noted on paper

Punctuation: correct errors noted on paper

Legibility: excellent   good   fair   poor

_____   excellent   good   fair   poor

_____   excellent   good   fair   poor

Strengths:

Weaknesses:

Comments/Suggestions:

LESSON TWENTY

Objectives
1. To demonstrate the ability to assess another's writing thorough a peer editing exercise
2. To demonstrate the ability to accept constructive criticism and make changes in their writing when necessary

Activity #1
    Put students in pairs for peer editing and give each student a peer evaluation form. Students will exchange their letters written in class the day before and make comments regarding content, language use, and conventions (under "Editor"). Students will return letters to the writer and then they respond to their peer's comments about their own writing on the editing sheet (under "Writer"). After thanking his/her peer for their comments, the writer will revise and rewrite the letter to turn in for a grade.

Activity #2
    Once students have edited and revised their writing, they may work on finishing their posters for the upcoming presentations or their character journals.

Editor's Name _____ Date_____

Writer's Name _____ Assignment_____

Peer Editing for Writing Assignments

   A. **Was the writer's position clearly stated?**

If your answer is "yes," be sure to tell the writer what he/she did that you especially liked. If your answer is "no," tell the writer what he/she could have included in order to write a better essay.

Editor: _____

_____

_____

Writer: _____

_____

_____

   B. **Did he/she provide enough details to support his/her position?**

If your answer is "yes," be sure to tell the writer what you especially liked about his/her response. If your answer is "no," you must tell the writer how he/she could improve his/her response (adding specific details that were missed, connecting to position better, or adding embedded quotations).

Editor: _____

_____

_____

Writer: _____

_____

_____

   C. **Identify sentence type**

Be sure to know the difference between simple, simple with compound subject, simple with compound predicate, compound, complex, and compound-complex. Using the first body paragraph, correctly identify each sentence type. If there is sufficient sentence structure variety, tell the writer what he/she did well. If not, explain what he/she could have done differently.

Sentence 1: _____   *Sentence 5:* _____

Sentence 2: _____   *Sentence 6:* _____

Sentence 3: _____   *Sentence 7:* _____

Sentence 4: _____   *Sentence 8:* _____

Editor: _____

_____

Writer: _____

_____

D. Address the Focus Correction Areas

Did the writer follow the specifics of the letter such as (address each individually):

Organization:

Editor: _____

Writer: _____

Use of vocabulary words as directed:

Editor: _____

Writer: _____

Cite novel:

Editor: _____

Writer: _____

E. Check for errors in grammar, spelling, punctuation, etc.

Editor: _____

Writer: _____

LESSONS TWENTY-ONE AND TWENTY TWO

<u>Objective</u>
To practice public speaking skills through presenting their research projects

<u>Activity</u>
Students will each give a 7-10 minute presentation on his/her gothic author, being sure to share all of the following:
- brief biographical sketch of the author
- brief summary of first story
- explanation of author's use of gothic elements in first story and how they were successful in creating a particular atmosphere
- brief summary of second story
- explanation of author's use of gothic elements in second story and how they were successful in creating a particular atmosphere
- author's contribution to the gothic genre

An evaluation sheet is included below for your convenience.

Presentation Evaluation Sheet

Name _____

Author: _____

Story #1: _____

Story #2: _____

Each of the following will be graded on a scale of 1-5, with 1 being the lowest; each is worth 20% of the overall grade.

Part I: Student provided an accurate biographical sketch of the author
Part II: Student provided brief and accurate summaries of the two stories
Part III: Student identified gothic elements in both stories and explained how their use was successful in creating a specific atmosphere
Part IV: Student provides information about author's contribution to the Gothic genre
Part V: Student has created a visual for his presentation (poster)

Part I: _____

Part II: _____

Part III: _____

Part IV: _____

Part V: _____

Total: _____   X Five   Total Grade: _____

Comments:

LESSON TWENTY-THREE

Objective
    To review the main events and ideas of *Dracula*

Activity
    Choose one of the review games/activities included in this packet and spend the remainder of your class time as outlined there.

REVIEW GAMES/ACTIVITIES *Dracula*

1. Ask the class to make up a unit test for *Dracula*. The test should have 4 sections: matching, true/false, short answer, and essay. Students may use 1/2 period to make the test and then swap papers and use the other 1/2 class period to take a test a classmate has devised. (open book) You may want to use the unit test included in this packet or take questions from the students' unit tests to formulate your own test.

2. Take 1/2 period for students to make up true and false questions (including the answers). Collect the papers and divide the class into two teams. Draw a big tic-tac-toe board on the chalk board. Make one team X and one team O. Ask questions to each side, giving each student one turn. If the question is answered correctly, that students' team's letter (X or O) is placed in the box. If the answer is incorrect, no letter is placed in the box. The object is to get three in a row like tic-tac-toe. You may want to keep track of the number of games won for each team.

3. Take 1/2 period for students to make up questions (true/false and short answer). Collect the questions. Divide the class into two teams. You'll alternate asking questions to individual members of teams A & B (like in a spelling bee). The question keeps going from A to B until it is correctly answered, then a new question is asked. A correct answer does not allow the team to get another question. Correct answers are +2 points; incorrect answers are -1 point.

4. Have students pair up and quiz each other from their study guides and class notes.

5. Give students a *Dracula* crossword puzzle to complete.

6. Divide your class into two teams. Use *Dracula* crossword words with their letters jumbled as a word list. Student 1 from Team A faces off against Student 1 from Team B. You write the first jumbled word on the board. The first student (1A or 1B) to unscramble the word wins the chance for his/her team to score points. If 1A wins the jumble, go to student 2A and give him/her a clue. He/she must give you the correct word which matches that clue. If he/she does, Team A scores a point, and you give student 3A a clue for which you expect another correct response. Continue giving Team A clues until some team member makes an incorrect response. An incorrect response sends the game back to the jumbled-word face off, this time with students 2A and 2B. Instead of repeating giving clues to the first few students of each team, continue with the student after the one who gave the last incorrect response on the team. For example, if Team B wins the jumbled-word face-off, and student 5B gave the last incorrect answer for Team B, you would

start this round of clue questions with student 6B, and so on. The team with the most points wins!

7. Play *What's My Line?*. This is similar to the old television show. Students assume the roles of different characters from the epic. One student gives clues to the class, or to a panel of contestants. The contestants try to guess the identity of the guest. Students may enjoy assisting you in creating rules and procedures for the game.

8. Play Jeopardy. Divide the class into two groups. Assign each group a category or book from the epic and have them devise answers for that category. Play the game according to the television show procedures.

9. Play Drawing in the Details. This is similar to Pictionary. Divide students into teams. A student from one team draws a scene from the epic. (You may want to specify the Book or section.) Drawings should be kept simple, to keep the pace lively. Students in the opposing team locate the scene in their books and read it aloud. If they are incorrect, the illustrator's team has a chance to guess. Involve students in setting up a scoring system and any other necessary rules.

LESSON TWENTY-FOUR

Objective
    To test the students understanding of the main ideas and themes in *Dracula*

Activity #1
    Distribute the unit tests. Go over the instructions in detail and allow the students the entire class period to complete the exam.

NOTES ABOUT THE UNIT TESTS IN THIS UNIT:

    There are 5 different unit tests which follow.
    There are two short answer tests which are based primarily on facts from the novel. The answer key for short answer unit test 1 follows the student test. The answer key for short answer test 2 follows the student short answer unit test 2.
    There is one advanced short answer unit test, and it is based on the extra discussion questions. Use the matching key for short answer unit test 1 to check the matching section of the advanced short answer unit test. There is no key for the short answer questions. The answers will be based on the discussions you have had during class.
    There are two multiple choice unit tests. Following the two unit tests, you will find an answer sheet on which students should mark their answers. The same answer sheet should be used for both tests; however, students' answers will be different for each test. Following the students' answer sheet for the multiple choice tests you will find your two keys: one for multiple choice test 1 and one for multiple choice test 2.
    The short answer tests have a vocabulary section. You should choose 10 of the vocabulary words from this unit, read them orally and have the students write them down. Then, either have students write a definition or use the words in sentences.

    Use these words for the vocabulary section of the advanced short answer unit test:

saturnine	voluptuous	expostulate	acquiesced
presage	subcutaneous	emaciated	physiognomist
mundane	abasement	remonstrance	enigmatical

Activity #2
    Collect all test papers and assigned books prior to the end of the class period.

UNIT TESTS

SHORT ANSWER UNIT TEST 1 - *Dracula*

I. Matching/Identify

____ 1. Arthur Holmwood   A. lawyer who traveled to Transylvania

____ 2. Jonathan Harker   B. died of fright after a wolf jumped in a window

____ 3. Quincey Morris   C. scarred by a communion wafer

____ 4. Lucy Westenra   D. allowed the Count to enter the asylum

____ 5. John Seward   E. an American from Texas

____ 6. Renfield   F. the "bloofer" lady

____ 7. Abraham Van Helsing   G. Lord Godalming

____ 8. Mina Murray   H. purchased various properties in England

____ 9. Mrs. Westenra   I. first to know what was wrong with Lucy

____ 10. Count Dracula   J. managed an insane asylum

II. Short Answer

1. Describe the driver who comes to meet Jonathan Harker at the Borgo Pass.

2. What is Jonathan Harker's occupation, and what is his purpose for coming to Transylvania?

3. Describe the patient who seems to be of most interest to Dr. Seward.

4. List the various "pets" that Renfield keeps and tell what he does with them.

5. According to the captain's addendum to the ship's log, what happens to the men on the Demeter?

6. What does Mina see in the moonlit churchyard when she goes looking for Lucy?

7. What action does Van Helsing believe is necessary to keep Lucy alive?

8. Describe how Lucy's soul is set free.

9. Why did Renfield become angry with the Count?

10. How is Count Dracula finally destroyed?

III. Essay

Dracula may be considered an epistolary novel. This means that the plot is revealed through a series of letters and diary entries. What makes this technique more effective as opposed to a third person account? From whose point of view is this novel presented (there are several)? How would a change of point of view affect the overall novel?

IV. Vocabulary

Write down the vocabulary words. Go back later and write down the correct definition for each word.

1.

2.

3.

4.

5.

6.

7.

8.

9.

10.

SHORT ANSWER UNIT TEST 1 ANSWER KEY – *Dracula*

I. Matching/Identify

G	1. Arthur Holmwood	A. lawyer who traveled to Transylvania
A	2. Jonathan Harker	B. died of fright after a wolf jumped in a window
E	3. Quincey Morris	C. scarred by a communion wafer
F	4. Lucy Westenra	D. allowed the Count to enter the asylum
J	5. John Seward	E. an American from Texas
D	6. Renfield	F. the "bloofer" lady
I	7. Abraham Van Helsing	G. Lord Godalming
C	8. Mina Murray	H. purchased various properties in England
B	9. Mrs. Westenra	I. first to know what was wrong with Lucy
H	10. Count Dracula	J. managed an insane asylum

II. Short Answer

1. Describe the driver who comes to meet Jonathan Harker at the Borgo Pass.
    He is tall and thin, dressed all in black, has a long brown beard and a black hat that hides his face completely. He is also very strong.

2. What is Jonathan Harker's occupation, and what is his purpose for coming to Transylvania?
    He is an attorney and has come to close a real estate transaction for a house in England that the Count purchased.

3. Describe the patient who seems to be of most interest to Dr. Seward.
    R. M. Renfield is about 59 years old, is very strong, and is extremely excitable. Dr. Seward thinks that he could be very dangerous.

4. List the various "pets" that Renfield keeps and tell what he does with them.
    Renfield catches flies, spiders and birds. He feeds the flies to the spiders, and he feeds the spiders to the birds. He also eats the flies and spiders.

5. According to the captain's addendum to the ship's log, what happens to the men on the Demeter?
    Men on the ship began to mysteriously disappear one by one.

6. What does Mina see in the moonlit churchyard when she goes looking for Lucy?
   Mina sees a dark, sinister figure bent over Lucy in the churchyard.

7. What action does Van Helsing believe is necessary to keep Lucy alive?
   Van Helsing believes that Lucy needs an immediate blood transfusion to save her life.

8. Describe how Lucy's soul is set free.
   Arthur hammers a wooden stake through her heart, and Van Helsing cuts off her head, and stuffs her mouth with garlic.

9. Why did Renfield become angry with the Count?
   Renfield realizes the Dracula only promised him lives just to gain entrance to the hospital so that the Count could get to Mina. The Count has lied and give Renfield nothing.

10. How is Count Dracula finally destroyed?
    Jonathan Harker slits the Count's throat with his Kukri knife and Quincey Morris stabs the Count in the chest. The Count turns to dust.

Parts III and IV:

For the essay portion, answers will vary. The vocabulary section will depend on which words you select from the list.

SHORT ANSWER UNIT TEST 2 - *Dracula*

I. Matching/Identify

____ 1. Lucy Westenra   A. lawyer who traveled to Transylvania

____ 2. Mina Murray   B. died of fright after a wolf jumped in a window

____ 3. Mrs. Westenra   C. scarred by a communion wafer

____ 4. Jonathan Harker   D. allowed the Count to enter the asylum

____ 5. Arthur Holmwood   E. an American from Texas

____ 6. Abraham Van Helsing   F. the "bloofer" lady

____ 7. Quincey Morris   G. Lord Godalming

____ 8. John Seward   H. purchased various properties in England

____ 9. Count Dracula   I. first to know what was wrong with Lucy

____ 10. Renfield   J. managed an insane asylum

II. Short Answer

1. What does the Count want Jonathan Harker to teach him while at Castle Dracula?

2. Jonathan Harker falls asleep in the parlor. What does he see upon waking?

3. Jonathan decides to climb the wall of the castle into the Count's room. Describe what Jonathan Harker discovers in the Count's room.

4. Describe Renfield's systematic way of collecting lives.

5. What request does Jonathan make of Mina regarding his notebook?

6. What did Dr. Seward and Van Helsing notice about Lucy's body when they went to pay their respects?

7. What strange occurrences began taking place in Hampstead not long after Lucy's funeral?

8. What limitations does Van Helsing say that a vampire has?

9. Describe the scene Van Helsing, Dr. Seward, Lord Godalming, and Quincey Morris witness after breaking down the door to the Harkers' bedroom.

10. How does the group divide its members in order to best capture the Count?

III. Composition

Fear is categorized as a negative emotion, yet many people seem to like to be scared. They seek thrill rides at amusement parks, go sky-diving, race cars, and watch horror movies. Those who read gothic literature (especially horror literature) fall into a similar category of those who seem to like to be scared. What possible attraction might all of these activities draw for people? How does *Dracula* satisfy this attraction?

IV. Vocabulary
	Write down the vocabulary words. Go back later and write down the correct definitions for the words.

1.

2.

3.

4.

5.

6.

7.

8.

9.

10.

ANSWER KEY: SHORT ANSWER UNIT TEST 2 - *Dracula*

I. Matching/Identify

F	1. Lucy Westenra	A.	lawyer who traveled to Transylvania
C	2. Mina Murray	B.	died of fright after a wolf jumped in a window
B	3. Mrs. Westenra	C.	scarred by a communion wafer
A	4. Jonathan Harker	D.	allowed the Count to enter the asylum
G	5. Arthur Holmwood	E.	an American from Texas
I	6. Abraham Van Helsing	F.	the "bloofer" lady
E	7. Quincey Morris	G.	Lord Godalming
J	8. John Seward	H.	purchased various properties in England
H	9. Count Dracula	I.	first to know what was wrong with Lucy
D	10. Renfield	J.	managed an insane asylum

II. Short Answer

1. What does the Count want Jonathan Harker to teach him while at Castle Dracula?
   The Count wants Jonathan Harker to teach him to speak English well enough that he would never be recognized as a foreigner.

2. Jonathan Harker falls asleep in the parlor. What does he see upon waking?
   Jonathan sees three beautiful, voluptuous women, with long sharp teeth, who try to seduce him.

3. Jonathan decides to climb the wall of the castle into the Count's room. Describe what Jonathan Harker discovers in the Count's room.
   The room is barely furnished with odd things, which seem to have never been used. In the corner is an unlocked heavy door that leads to an old, ruined chapel, which had evidently been a graveyard. The wooden boxes that had been delivered were filled with earth, and the Count was in a box on top of one of the piles of freshly dug earth. The Count's eyes were open, but they did not seem to register Jonathan's presence. Jonathan wanted to look for a key, but he lost his nerve.

4. Describe Renfield's systematic way of collecting lives.
    Renfield believes that one spider that eats many flies contains many lives. The bird that eats spiders that have eaten flies contains more lives. He who eats the bird ingests all of those lives.

5. What request does Jonathan make of Mina regarding his notebook?
    He tells her to keep the notebook and read it if she wants to, but she must never tell him what is on the pages unless some extreme emergency were to arise that would force him to look back on what had happened.

6. What did Dr. Seward and Van Helsing notice about Lucy's body when they went to pay their respects?
    Lucy looked more beautiful in death, and she seemed so life-like.

7. What strange occurrences began taking place in Hampstead not long after Lucy's funeral?
    Children are mysteriously disappearing and later reappearing, claiming that they were playing with a "bloofer lady."

8. What limitations does Van Helsing say that a vampire has?
    a. no food but blood
    b. no shadow or reflection
    c. cannot enter a place unless invited to do so
    d. no daytime powers
    e. cannot pass over running water except at high and low tides
    f. repulsed by garlic and sacred objects (crucifixes, the Host, etc)

9. Describe the scene Van Helsing, Dr. Seward, Lord Godalming, and Quincey Morris witness after breaking down the door to the Harker's bedroom.
    Jonathan Harker was in a sound, drug-like sleep, and Mina was in a trance. The Count was standing over Mina, forcing her to drink his blood from an open wound in his chest.

10. How does the group divide its members in order to best capture the Count?
    Arthur and Jonathan will take a steamboat and attempt to locate the boat that Dracula is on. Dr. Seward and Quincey Morris will travel along the riverbank on horseback to make sure the Count doesn't get on land. Mina and Van Helsing will go directly to Castle Dracula to destroy his lair.

Parts III and IV:
For the essay portion, answers will vary. The vocabulary section will depend on which words you select from the list.

ADVANCED SHORT ANSWER TEST – *Dracula*

I. Matching/Identify

   ____ 1. Arthur Holmwood   A. lawyer who traveled to Transylvania

   ____ 2. Jonathan Harker   B. died of fright after a wolf jumped in a window

   ____ 3. Quincey Morris   C. scarred by a communion wafer

   ____ 4. Lucy Westenra   D. allowed the Count to enter the asylum

   ____ 5. John Seward   E. an American from Texas

   ____ 6. Renfield   F. the "bloofer" lady

   ____ 7. Abraham Van Helsing   G. Lord Godalming

   ____ 8. Mina Murray   H. purchased various properties in England

   ____ 9. Mrs. Westenra   I. first to know what was wrong with Lucy

   ____ 10. Count Dracula   J. managed an insane asylum

II. Short Answer

   1. Why do Van Helsing, Dr. Seward, and Quincey Morris vow never to tell Arthur about the fact that they, too, gave blood to Lucy through transfusion?

   2. Why does Dracula entice Renfield with the promise of many lives? What does he want from Renfield?

3. Discuss three specific character traits for each of the following: Jonathan Harker, Mina Harker, Van Helsing, Count Dracula. Support the traits with evidence from the text.

4. Discuss how each of the following 19th century topics was presented in Bram Stoker's *Dracula*.
    a. The Development of Psychoanalysis

    b. Gender roles in Victorian Society

    c. Changes in Medicine/Science

    d. Superstition

5. Tell at least four elements of gothic literature and explain how each is used in *Dracula*.

6. Note that both Count Dracula and Renfield mention that drinking blood will bring eternal life. Discuss how this could be a twisted parallel to the Christian practice of Holy Communion. Why is it significant that Renfield does not want to be responsible for the souls of the creatures he eats? How does that create a contrast for Count Dracula?

7. Note that it is Van Helsing's use of the consecrated Communion wafer that both destroys Dracula's lair and protects him from harm. What might be Bram Stoker's view of religion based on this detail?

8. Suppose Lucy had decided to accept Dr. Seward's proposal of marriage. Would that choice have affected Arthur's or Quincey's roles in her redemption? What if she had chosen Quincey Morris?

9. For each of the following characters, select an object and explain how that object could be used to symbolize that person's particular character traits:
   a. Abraham Van Helsing

   b. Lucy Westenra

   c. Mina Harker

   d. Renfield

   e. Count Dracula

III. Composition

Thinking back over the classroom presentations about short stories in the gothic genre, examine what archetypal characters seem to appear over and over again (such as the Damsel in Distress, the Gallant but Tormented Hero, The Evil Villain/Monster that comes in a variety of forms: vampires, wolfmen, "created" creatures, ghosts, etc.). How did the various authors from the class presentations present these archetypes yet still manage to create a unique story? How did Bram Stoker use these archetypes in *Dracula*?

IV. Vocabulary
    A. Listen to the vocabulary words and write them here. Go back and write a definition for each.

1.

2.

3.

4.

5.

6.

7.

8.

9.

10.

11.

12.

    B. For the following topic, include at least five of the vocabulary words in your response.

What influence of gothic literature can be found in today's movies? Video games? Could they be truly categorized as "Gothic"? Why or why not?

MULTIPLE CHOICE UNIT TEST 1 - *Dracula*

I. Matching

____ 1. Arthur Holmwood   A. lawyer who traveled to Transylvania

____ 2. Jonathan Harker   B. died of fright after a wolf jumped in a window

____ 3. Quincey Morris   C. scarred by a communion wafer

____ 4. Lucy Westenra   D. allowed the Count to enter the asylum

____ 5. John Seward   E. an American from Texas

____ 6. Renfield   F. the "bloofer" lady

____ 7. Abraham Van Helsing G. Lord Goldalming

____ 8. Mina Murray   H. purchased various properties in England

____ 9. Mrs. Westenra   I. first to know what was wrong with Lucy

____ 10. Count Dracula   J. managed an insane asylum

II. Multiple Choice

1. What does Jonathan Harker find waiting for him when he arrives at the Golden Krone Hotel?
    a. His fiancée Mina arrived to surprise him.
    b. There is a letter from Count Dracula.
    c. There is a coach waiting to take him to his final destination.
    d. There is a letter from his fiancée Mina.

2. What does Jonathan find strange about his carriage ride to Castle Dracula?
    a. It is cold outside, but Jonathan stays warm in the carriage.
    b. Jonathan feels they are traveling over and over the same ground.
    c. The carriage driver will not talk to Jonathan.
    d. Jonathan keeps falling asleep.

3. Who are the "children of the night?"
    a. the homeless children wandering the streets
    b. the bats that fly in large winding circles above the trees
    c. the howling wolves
    d. the souls of the recently departed

4. What did Jonathan Harker notice is absent from every room he enteres in Dracula's castle?
    a. books
    b. mirrors
    c. candles
    d. pictures

5. What does the Count warn Jonathan against before he leaves for the night?
    a. He tells Jonathan to be careful while wandering outdoors.
    b. He tells Jonathan not to fall asleep with a candle burning.
    c. He tells Jonathan not to fall asleep in any room other than his own.
    d. He tells Jonathan not to trust anyone who comes to the castle.

6. Who is Quincey Morris?
    a. He is Lucy's brother.
    b. He is Arthur Holmwood's friend.
    c. He is Mina's father.
    d. He is Jonathan Harker's employer.

7. What is the name of the patient who seems to be of most interest to Dr. Seward?
    a. Jonathan Harker
    b. Quincey Morris
    c. Renfield
    d. Mrs. Westenra

8. What does Renfield do that disgusts Dr. Seward?
    a. He captures flies and feeds them to spiders.
    b. He laps water from a dish like a dog.
    c. He bites at his own flesh and sucks the blood.
    d. He eats live creatures.

9. According to the captain's addendum to the ship's log, what happened to the men on the *Demeter*?
    a. The men went insane one by one and jumped off the ship.
    b. The men ate rotten food, got sick and died.
    c. The men went insane and killed one another.
    d. The men begun to disappear one by one.

10. What does Mina see in the moonlit churchyard when she goes looking for Lucy?
    a. Mina sees a dark, sinister figure bent over Lucy.
    b. Mina sees a large dog.
    c. Mina sees a large bat circling over her head.
    d. Mina sees Lucy ready to fling herself from the cliff.

11. What request does Jonathan make of Mina regarding his notebook?
    a. He wants her to read it so that she will understand what he's been through.
    b. He wants her to burn it.
    c. He wants her to keep it in a safe place and read it only if she wants to.
    d. He wants her to pass it on to Dr. Seward to help with Lucy's condition.

12. What does Mina do with Jonathan's notebook?
    a. She reads it and is horrified.
    b. She burns it.
    c. She wraps it and ties it with ribbon as a wedding gift to Jonathan.
    d. She gives it to Dr. Seward.

13. What action does Van Helsing believe is necessary to keep Lucy alive?
    a. chemotherapy
    b. a tight tourniquet around the wound on her throat to keep it from bleeding
    c. angioplasty
    d. a blood transfusion

14. What happens to Lucy's mother?
    a. She dies of a heart attack when a wolf jumps through Lucy's window.
    b. She leaves the country because her health is failing so badly.
    c. She is hospitalized after collapsing in Lucy's room.
    d. She falls down the stairs when she is trying to get help for Lucy.

15. What is Renfield's reaction when some men remove several heavy boxes from Carfax?
    a. He attacksd them.
    b. He attempts to help them move the boxes.
    c. He wants to know where the boxes are being taken.
    d. He suddenly becomes very frightened.

16. What does Van Helsing want to do with Lucy's body?
    a. burn it
    b. bury it in consecrated soil as soon as possible
    c. cut off the head, and take out her heart
    d. douse it with holy water and place the Host in her mouth

17. Who is Lord Godalming?
    a. It is Quincey Morris's real title.
    b. He owns the Westenra home; he wants to foreclose on it.
    c. It is Arthur Holmwood's title after the death of his father.
    d. He is a patient of Dr. Seward's.

18. What does Jonathan Harker see that causes him to go pale as he walks down Piccadilly?
    a. He sees Count Dracula, even though he looks younger.
    b. He sees Lucy with a child.
    c. He sees Mina with another man.
    d. He sees a wolf tear a man's throat out.

19. How does Van Helsing explain the bite marks found on the children of Hampstead Heath?
    a. He claims that a bat made them
    b. He claims that Lucy made them.
    c. He claims that a wolf made them.
    d. He claims that a large dog made them.

20. Who strikes the blow that sets Lucy's soul free?
    a. Van Helsing
    b. Quincey Morris
    c. Dr. Seward
    d. Arthur Holmwood

21. Renfield says that he wants life from other beings, but he does not want something else. What is it he does **not** want?
    a. their souls
    b. to have vengeance taken against him
    c. to have to give these lives to the Master
    d. to share life with anyone else

22. Why does Renfield become angry with the Count?
    a. Renfield wants total control of London, not shared control with the Count.
    b. Renfield knows that he cannot have Lucy because she has been destroyed.
    c. The Count promised to release him from the asylum but didn't.
    d. He realized the Count has lied and used him to get to Mina Harker.

23. How does Van Helsing propose to enter the Count's locked house in Piccadilly by daylight without drawing unnecessary attention?
    a. He will pretend to be a contractor who is renovating the house.
    b. Arthur will create a diversion and Van Helsing will break in the back door.
    c. Arthur and Quincey will pretend to be the owner and hire a locksmith.
    d. He will call the real estate company and tell them he is a relative of the owner.

24. How did the Count find out that Van Helsing and the others were chasing him?
    a. Czarina Catherine tells him.
    b. He changes into a bat and sees them pursuing him.
    c. His spies tell him.
    d. He is mentally linked to Mina, and he can read her mind.

III. Composition

1. Why do Van Helsing, Dr. Seward, and Quincey Morris vow never to tell Arthur about the fact that they, too, gave blood to Lucy through transfusion?

2. Why does Dracula entice Renfield with the promise of many lives? What does he want from Renfield?

3. When the vampire Lucy is to be destroyed, why is it significant that Arthur is the one to strike the blow that sets her free? What comments on female sexuality in the Victorian era might Stoker have been making in this scene?

4. Tell at least four elements of gothic literature and explain how each is used in *Dracula*.

5. Note that both Count Dracula and Renfield mention that drinking blood will bring eternal life. Discuss how this could be a twisted parallel to the Christian practice of Holy Communion. Why is it significant that Renfield does not want to be responsible for the souls of the creatures he eats? How does that create a contrast for Count Dracula?

IV. Vocabulary - Match the correct definitions to the words.

____ 1. polyglot   A. yielded to an overwhelming desire; gave up or gave in

____ 2. voluptuous   B. an occupation, especially one for which a person is suited

____ 3. instigation   C. adopting the customs and attitudes of the prevailing culture

____ 4. succumbed   D. beginning again

____ 5. obliterated   E. to strike down or hit

____ 6. maelstrom   F. speaking, writing, written in, or composed of several languages

____ 7. anguid   G. a violent or turbulent situation: a large violent whirlpool

____ 8. vocation   H. extreme or unnatural paleness

____ 9. converged   I. murderous

____ 10. pallor   J. deliberate and intentional triggering of trouble or discord

____ 11. verbatim   K. indicative of or announcing something to come

____ 12. smote   L. having bounds; limited

____ 13. tacit   M. lacking energy or vitality; weak

____ 14. assimilation N. not spoken

____ 15. homicidal   O. causing annoyance, weariness, or vexation

____ 16. resumption   P. arising from the satisfaction of sensual desires

____ 17. heraldic   Q. came together from different directions; met

____ 18. wily   R. in exactly the same words; word for word

____ 19. finite   S. marked by skill in deception

____ 20. irksome   T. to do away with completely so as to leave no trace

MULTIPLE CHOICE UNIT TEST 2 - *Dracula*

I. Matching

____ 1. Lucy Westenra   A. lawyer who traveled to Transylvania

____ 2. Mina Murray   B. died of fright after a wolf jumped in a window

____ 3. Mrs. Westenra   C. scarred by a communion wafer

____ 4. Jonathan Harker   D. allowed the Count to enter the asylum

____ 5. Arthur Holmwood   E. an American from Texas

____ 6. Abraham Van Helsing   F. the "bloofer" lady

____ 7. Quincey Morris   G. Lord Godalming

____ 8. John Seward   H. purchased various properties in England

____ 9. Count Dracula   I. first to know what was wrong with Lucy

____ 10. Renfield   J. managed an insane asylum

II. Multiple Choice

1. At the opening of the novel, where is Jonathan Harker going?
    a. to Lucy Wistenra's vacation home in Whitby
    b. to meet with his mentor, Professor Van Helsing in Amsterdam
    c. home to London after a long business trip
    d. to Transylvania to meet with a client

2. Why does the hotel landlady beg Jonathan not to continue his journey?
    a. It is the Eve of St. George's Day, and at midnight all evil things will have full sway.
    b. It is a full moon and at midnight all evil things will have full sway.
    c. She begs him to wait until the weather is better.
    d. She begs him to stay with her to protect her from the Count.

3. What does Jonathan find strange about his carriage ride to Castle Dracula?
    a. It is cold outside, but Jonathan stays warm in the carriage.
    b. Jonathan feels they are traveling over and over the same ground.
    c. The carriage driver will not talk to Jonathan.
    d. Jonathan keeps falling asleep.

4. Who are the "children of the night?"
    a. the homeless children wandering the streets
    b. the bats that fly in large winding circles above the trees
    c. the howling wolves
    d. the souls of the recently departed

5. When Jonathan Harker looks in his shaving mirror, what peculiar thing does he notice about the Count?
    a. The Count has no reflection in the mirror.
    b. The Count has not changed clothes since the night before.
    c. The Count seems paler than he was on the previous evening.
    d. The Count appears to have grown younger.

6. Jonathan Harker falls asleep in the parlor. What does he see upon waking?
    a. A large wolf has gotten into the castle and is staring hungrily at Jonathan.
    b. He sees three beautiful women who try to seduce him.
    c. He sees the Count coming out from a secret chamber hidden behind the wall.
    d. He sees the lights flicker strangely as a storm brews outside.

7. Jonathan decides to climb the wall of the castle into the Count's room. Which of these things does he not find in the Counts rooms?
    a. an old ruined chapel
    b. boxes filled with dirt
    c. the Count
    d. a key

8. Who is Quincey Morris?
    a. He is Lucy's brother.
    b. He is Arthur Holmwood's friend.
    c. He is Mina's father.
    d. He is Jonathan Harker's employer.

9. What request does Jonathan make of Mina regarding his notebook?
    a. He wants her to read it so that she will understand what he's been through.
    b. He wants her to burn it.
    c. He wants her to keep it in a safe place and read it only if she wants to.
    d. He wants her to pass it on to Dr. Seward to help with Lucy's condition.

10. Arthur Holmwood asks Dr. Seward to examine Lucy. What are Dr. Seward's findings regarding Lucy?
    a. He thinks that she has a rare blood disease.
    b. He finds that her muscles are beginning to deteriorate.
    c. He finds nothing at all to be concerned about.
    d. He can not find any functional disturbance, but is concerned about her weakness and appearance.

11. What specific instructions does Van Helsing give Dr. Seward regarding Lucy before he leaves for Amsterdam?
    a. to make sure she gets up and walks every hour to increase circulation
    b. to be sure she eats at least five small meals a day
    c. to never leave her unattended for any reason
    d. to make sure she drinks at least sixty-four ounces of water daily

12. What is in the package that Van Helsing receives from abroad?
    a. garlic flowers
    b. tulips
    c. pieces of the Host (consecrated communion wafers)
    d. a medical journal to help him in his treatment of Lucy

13. What does Mrs. Westenra tell Van Helsing that causes him to break down in tears?
    a. Lucy is dead.
    b. Mina is severely ill just as Lucy is.
    c. She threw away the flowers in Lucy's bedroom and opened the windows.
    d. Dr. Seward had just come down with the same illness as Lucy.

14. What happens to Lucy's mother?
    a. She dies of a heart attack when a wolf jumps through Lucy's window.
    b. She leaves the country because her health is failing so badly.
    c. She is hospitalized after collapsing in Lucy's room.
    d. She falls down the stairs when she is trying to get help for Lucy.

15. What ultimately becomes of Lucy Westenra?
    a. Dr. Van Helsing is able to find a cure for her.
    b. She marries Arthur Holmwood.
    c. She dies.
    d. She breaks her engagement to Arthur Holmwood and marries Quincey Morris.

16. What does Jonathan Harker see that causes him to go pale as he walks down Piccadilly?
    a. He sees Count Dracula, even though he looks younger.
    b. He sees Lucy with a child.
    c. He sees Mina with another man.
    d. He sees a wolf tear a man's throat out.

17. Van Helsing is trying to make Dr. Seward accept and understand Lucy's death and what is happening to the children of Hampstead. Which of the following is not one of the unexplained mysteries of the natural world that Van Helsing uses in his explanation?
    a. There are bats that exist that drain the blood of cattle and horses.
    b. There are such tortured souls that live as vampires throughout centuries.
    c. Tortoises, elephants and parrots live longer than generations of men.
    d. The Indian fakir can rise from the dead after several years.

18. What do Van Helsing and Dr. Seward find when they first opened Lucy's coffin?
    a. Lucy looks more beautiful than ever.
    b. It is empty.
    c. Her body is beginning to deteriorate.
    d. Someone has filled it with dirt.

19. What is Arthur's reaction when Lucy speaks to him in the cemetery?
    a. Arthur is overcome with grief and falls to the ground.
    b. Arthur is happy to see Lucy and runs to her.
    c. Arthur is mesmerized; he goes to Lucy as if in a trance.
    d. Arthur is frightened and runs from the cemetery.

20. Who do the realtors at Mitchell, Sons, and Candy claim purchased the house in Piccadilly?
    a. Count Dracula
    b. Lucy
    c. Lord Godalming
    d. Count DeVille

21. What does Count Dracula promise Renfield in exchange for letting him into the asylum?
    a. the lives of rats
    b. Mina Harker as his own
    c. the vampire Lucy as a life partner
    d. to share power in their conquest of London

22. What happens as a result of Van Helsing's attempt to protect Mina from the Count while they are gone?
    a. She screams at the sight of a crucifix.
    b. Her forehead is badly burned and scarred.
    c. She cannot bear the smell of garlic and refuses to wear the flowers.
    d. She is insulted that he would think she was becoming a vampire.

23. What single word does Mina hesitate to write in her journal?
    a. "drink"
    b. "pray"
    c. "death"
    d. "vampire"

24. How is Count Dracula finally destroyed?
    a. Arthur cuts off his head while Quincey Morris drives a wooden stake in his heart. They then stuff his mouth with garlic.
    b. Dr. Seward, Quincey Morris, Arthur, and Jonathan surround him with holy objects. The Count is surrounded and turns to dust.
    c. The men open his box and expose him to the sun, which turns him to dust.
    d. Jonathan slits his throat while Quincey Morris stabs him in the heart.

III. Composition

1. Van Helsing tells Dr. Seward the he must return to Amsterdam to think. What is it he needs to think about? What clues does Bram Stoker give the reader about Van Helsing and his studies?

2. Where is the climax of this novel? Explain your choice.

3. Why does Renfield turn against Count Dracula?

4. Note that it is Van Helsing's use of the consecrated Communion wafer that both destroys Dracula's lair and protects him from harm. What might be Bram Stoker's view of religion based on this detail?

5. How might the character of Arthur have been different if Van Helsing, Quincey Morris, and Dr. Seward told him that they, too, had given blood transfusions to Lucy?

IV. Vocabulary - Match the correct definitions to the words.

____ 1. caleche   A. extremely thin, especially as a result of starvation

____ 2. alacrity   B. characteristics of a scholar or thinker

____ 3. menial   C. a light carriage with low wheels and a collapsible top

____ 4. obeisance   D. located or placed just beneath the skin

____ 5. imperturbable   E. gesture, such as a curtsy, that expresses deference or respect

____ 6. acquiesce   F. to consent or comply passively or without protest

____ 7. apathy   G. to take in by deceptive means; deceive

____ 8. queried   H. cheerful willingness; eagerness; speed or quickness

____ 9. subcutaneous   I. lack of interest or concern, lack of emotion or feeling

____ 10. emaciated   J. appearing worn and exhausted

____ 11. tumult   K. set free or kept free from restrictions or bonds

____ 12. repudiated   L. questioned; inquired

____ 13. sophistic   M. long narrow opening; a crack or cleft

____ 14. unfettered   N. unshakably calm and collected

____ 15. lair   O. in a state of profound awe and respect and often love

____ 16. reverently   P. rejected emphatically as unfounded, untrue, or unjust

____ 17. haggard   Q. restraint for holding an animal in place

____ 18. fissure   R. relating to work or a job regarded as for a servant

____ 19. hoodwink   S. the den or dwelling of a wild animal; a hideaway

____ 20. tether   T. agitation of the mind or emotions

ANSWER SHEET - *Dracula*
Multiple Choice Unit Tests

I. Matching	II. Multiple Choice	IV. Vocabulary
1. ___	1. ___	1. ___
2. ___	2. ___	2. ___
3. ___	3. ___	3. ___
4. ___	4. ___	4. ___
5. ___	5. ___	5. ___
6. ___	6. ___	6. ___
7. ___	7. ___	7. ___
8. ___	8. ___	8. ___
9. ___	9. ___	9. ___
10. ___	10. ___	10. ___
	11. ___	11. ___
	12. ___	12. ___
	13. ___	13. ___
	14. ___	14. ___
	15. ___	15. ___
	16. ___	16. ___
	17. ___	17. ___
	18. ___	18. ___
	19. ___	19. ___
	20. ___	20. ___
	21. ___	
	22. ___	
	23. ___	
	24. ___	

ANSWER KEY - *Dracula*
Multiple Choice Unit Test 1

I. Matching	II. Multiple Choice	IV. Vocabulary
1. G	1. B	1. F
2. A	2. B	2. P
3. E	3. C	3. J
4. F	4. B	4. A
5. J	5. C	5. T
6. D	6. B	6. G
7. I	7. C	7. M
8. C	8. D	8. B
9. B	9. D	9. Q
10. H	10. A	10. H
	11. C	11. R
	12. C	12. E
	13. D	13. N
	14. A	14. C
	15. A	15. I
	16. C	16. D
	17. C	17. K
	18. A	18. S
	19. B	19. L
	20. D	20. O
	21. C	
	22. D	
	23. C	
	24. D	

ANSWER KEY - *Dracula*
Multiple Choice Unit Test 2

I. Matching	II. Multiple Choice	IV. Vocabulary
1. F	1. D	1. C
2. C	2. A	2. H
3. B	3. B	3. R
4. A	4. C	4. E
5. G	5. A	5. N
6. I	6. B	6. F
7. E	7. D	7. I
8. J	8. B	8. L
9. H	9. C	9. D
10. D	10. D	10. A
	11. C	11. T
	12. A	12. P
	13. C	13. B
	14. A	14. K
	15. C	15. S
	16. A	16. O
	17. B	17. J
	18. B	18. M
	19. C	19. G
	20. D	20. Q
	21. A	
	22. B	
	23. D	
	24. D	

UNIT RESOURCE MATERIALS

BULLETIN BOARD IDEAS - *Dracula*

1. Save one corner of the board for the best of students' *Dracula* writing assignments.

2. Take one of the word search puzzles from the extra activities packet and with a marker copy it over in a large size on the bulletin board. Write the clue words to find to one side. Invite students prior to and after class to find the words and circle them on the bulletin board.

3. Write several of the most significant quotations from the book onto the board on brightly colored paper.

4. Make a bulletin board listing the vocabulary words for this unit. As you complete sections of the novel and discuss the vocabulary for each section, write the definitions on the bulletin board. (If your board is one students face frequently, it will help them learn the words.)

5. Display the posters from the 19th Century Ideas and Concepts projects.

6. Create a compare and contrast bulletin board for fairy tales, focusing on their Gothic elements.

7. Display the students' captioned drawings based on Stoker's images from *Dracula*.

8. Display the characterization posters completed by the students.

9. Create a Gothic Authors bulletin board using the authors selected by students for their research projects.

10. Display the students' tombstones after sharing their poetic epitaphs.

11. Display the captioned drawings based on the images students' explored in Graveyard Poetry.

12. Display the students' character journals.

13. Create a Famous Monsters of Filmland bulletin board.

EXTRA ACTIVITIES - *Dracula*

One of the difficulties in teaching a novel is that all students don't read at the same speed. One student who likes to read may take the book home and finish it in a day or two. Sometimes a few students finish the in-class assignments early. The problem, then, is finding suitable extra activities for students.

One thing that seems to help is to keep a little library in the classroom. For this unit on *Dracula*, you might check out from the school library: Mary Shelley's *Frankenstein*, Robert Louis Stevenson's *Dr. Jekyll and Mr. Hyde*, Oscar Wilde's *The Picture of Dorian Gray* or *The Canterville Ghost*, Jane Austin's *Northanger Abbey,* Emily Bronte's *Wuthering Heights*, or H. G. Wells' *Time Machine* or *The Invisible Man.* Any stories or articles about the Industrial Revolution, the development of psychoanalysis, Victorian culture, or any stories carrying a gothic theme might also be of interest.

Other things you may keep on hand are puzzles. We have made some relating directly to *Dracula* for you. Feel free to duplicate them for your students to use.

Some students may like to draw. You might devise a contest or allow some extra-credit grade for students who draw characters or scenes from *Dracula*. Note, too, that if the students do not want to keep their drawings you may pick up some extra bulletin board materials this way. If you have a contest and you supply the prize (a CD or something like that perhaps), you could, possibly, make the drawing itself a non-returnable entry fee.

The pages which follow contain games, puzzles and worksheets. The keys, when appropriate, immediately follow the puzzle or worksheet. There are two main groups of activities: one group for the unit; that is, generally relating to *Dracula* text, and another group of activities related strictly to *Dracula* vocabulary.

Directions for these games, puzzles and worksheets are self-explanatory. The object here is to provide you with extra materials you may use in any way you choose.

MORE ACTIVITIES - *Dracula*

1. Have students work together to make a time line chronology of the events in the story. Take a large piece of construction paper and on one wall (or however you can physically arrange it in your room), make the events of the story along it. Students may want to add drawings or cut-out pictures to represent the events (as well as a written statement).

2. Have students design a book cover (front and back and inside flaps) for *Dracula*.

3. Have students design a bulletin board (ready to be put up; not just sketched) for *Dracula*.

4. Have students choose one chapter of the book and rewrite the journal entries, incorporating dialogue, as a play. In conjunction with this assignment, have students write a composition explaining the difficulties they encountered in changing from one written form to another.

5. From two or more film versions of *Dracula*, play the same scene as depicted by the different directors. Have students analyze the use of lighting, costumes, music, sets, make-up, and characterization. Decide which seems to be truer to Bram Stoker's novel and explain why.

6. Select another film in the horror genre and analyze it for the director's use of gothic elements (lighting, costumes/make-up, special effects, sound, characterization).

7. Have students create a bulletin board size map of England and northern Europe and outline the journeys of Count Dracula.

Dracula Word List

No.	Word	Clue/Definition
1.	ATTILA	Count Dracula claims to be a descendant of ___ the Hun.
2.	BACK	Renfield's is broken.
3.	BAT	Mina saw one flitting in the moonlight.
4.	BITE	These marks were found on the childrens' throats.
5.	BLOOD	Renfield laps the Doctor's off of the floor like a dog.
6.	BOXES	The Slovaks deliver large, wooden ___ with rope handles to the castle.
7.	BRIDES	The Three voluptuous women are the ___ of Dracula.
8.	BURIAL	Mina asks Jonathan to read the ___ Service for the Dead to her.
9.	CAPTAIN	The body of the ___ was tied to the wheel of the ship.
10.	CARFAX	Dracula owns ___, which is next door to Dr. Seward's place.
11.	CHILD	Jonathan hears the wail of a half-smothered ___ come from the bag.
12.	CRUCIFIX	Hotel landlady gives Jonathan this for protection
13.	DOG	A large one jumps off the ship and disappears in the dark.
14.	DRINK	Renfield stops himself before uttering this word.
15.	DUST	The purified vampires turn to this.
16.	ENGLISH	The Count wants Jonathan to teach him this.
17.	EVIL	At midnight on St. George's Day all ___ things in the world have full sway.
18.	FLOWERS	Mrs. Westerna throws away Lucy's garlic ___.
19.	GODALMING	Arthur Holmwood: Lord ___
20.	HARKER	He travels to Castle Dracula to meet with the Count about real estate.
21.	HEAD	Van Helsing wants to cut off Lucy's ___ and take out her heart.
22.	HELSING	He suggests that Lucy needs blood transfusions: Van ___
23.	HOLMWOOD	Lucy accepts his marriage proposal.
24.	HOST	Communion wafer used as a weapon against vampires
25.	LIVES	Renfield collects them.
26.	LUCY	She received 3 marriage proposals in one day.
27.	MASTER	Renfield's name for the Count
28.	MINA	She is engaged to marry Jonathan.
29.	MIND	The Count's is linked to Mina's.
30.	MIRRORS	There are none of these in the castle.
31.	NOSFERATU	The Un-Dead
32.	NOTEBOOK	Mina promises not to tell Jonathan about the contents of his ___ unless it becomes necessary.
33.	PIN	Mina thinks she accidentally pricked Lucy with one.
34.	QUINCY	American friend of Arthur Holmwood
35.	RATS	Dracula promises Renfield the lives of ___.
36.	REFLECTION	The Count has no ___ in Jonathan's mirror.
37.	SEWARD	Van Helsing instructs him to sit with Lucy through the night without leaving her.
38.	SOULS	Renfield wants life from other beings, not ___.
39.	STAKE	One is driven through Lucy's heart.
40.	STRENGTH	Jonathan marvels at the caleche driver's
41.	SUNRISE	Renfield is quiet from moonrise to ___.
42.	THREE	Number of letters the Count instructs Jonathan to write home
43.	TIGER	Van Helsing compares Dracula to one.
44.	TOMBSTONES	The old man claims these in the graveyard lie.
45.	TRANSYLVANIA	Count Dracula's home
46.	VAMPIRE	Dracula or Lucy, for example
47.	VARNA	Home port of the Demeter
48.	WESTERNA	Lucy's mother: Mrs. ___
49.	WINDOW	The Count escapes capture at Piccadilly by jumping out of this.
50.	WOLVES	Children of the Night

Dracula Word Search

```
P M P N P Q X H W G C R U C I F I X V L G
R N G L D R B F O O P H B R R B D V L Z J
V E T C J Q F F L D X K G K J P C C Y F T
M T F D X U T C V A M K G M N P A K W D B
D F Q L R I J G E L T L Z I B P E N Z Q G
S C Y R E N S V S M L G B N T R V I W F K
V M L J T C B U R I A L V A M P I R E C S
Q S Q H R Y T H V N M J I I T B L D A F Z
K P B E B B B I K G V N D N H T Q B E Y F
K L G S F L S Y O Q W H O A F N I X X S F
P I N Z B O Z L D N Y N G V R O G L T F S
T M C S U O C R L L S D U L J T T A A L T
W A R L N D A H I I D D T Y W E R H P O D
J S S W M W S T H V A C A S M B W M R W G
P T J N E I H R C E V A R N A O B I T E S
Q E S S L S R A H S X R E A L O H O S R E
T R V G Y Y T R R Q J F F R Q K M I X S T
V B N H Z G Q E O K H A S T K B R G X E Z
W E M I N D C L R R E X O G S N B X N Y S
K G K V M D N Q F N S R N T U F D F C B R
P Z K R N U W R Q J A I O S F T Z U K T J
Z N S W N S D L K Z S N P Z G T L C V V B
H O S T S T M R B L E W I N D O W W L Z D
S T R E N G T H E S B Z Z T S T K Y Y B T
D O O W M L O H W R V L F S T A K E S N W
```

ATTILA	CHILD	HEAD	NOSFERATU	SUNRISE
BACK	CRUCIFIX	HELSING	NOTEBOOK	THREE
BAT	DOG	HOLMWOOD	PIN	TIGER
BITE	DRINK	HOST	QUINCY	TOMBSTONES
BLOOD	DUST	LIVES	RATS	TRANSYLVANIA
BOXES	ENGLISH	LUCY	REFLECTION	VAMPIRE
BRIDES	EVIL	MASTER	SEWARD	VARNA
BURIAL	FLOWERS	MINA	SOULS	WESTERNA
CAPTAIN	GODALMING	MIND	STAKE	WINDOW
CARFAX	HARKER	MIRRORS	STRENGTH	WOLVES

Dracula Word Search Answer Key

ATTILA	CHILD	HEAD	NOSFERATU	SUNRISE
BACK	CRUCIFIX	HELSING	NOTEBOOK	THREE
BAT	DOG	HOLMWOOD	PIN	TIGER
BITE	DRINK	HOST	QUINCY	TOMBSTONES
BLOOD	DUST	LIVES	RATS	TRANSYLVANIA
BOXES	ENGLISH	LUCY	REFLECTION	VAMPIRE
BRIDES	EVIL	MASTER	SEWARD	VARNA
BURIAL	FLOWERS	MINA	SOULS	WESTERNA
CAPTAIN	GODALMING	MIND	STAKE	WINDOW
CARFAX	HARKER	MIRRORS	STRENGTH	WOLVES

Dracula Crossword

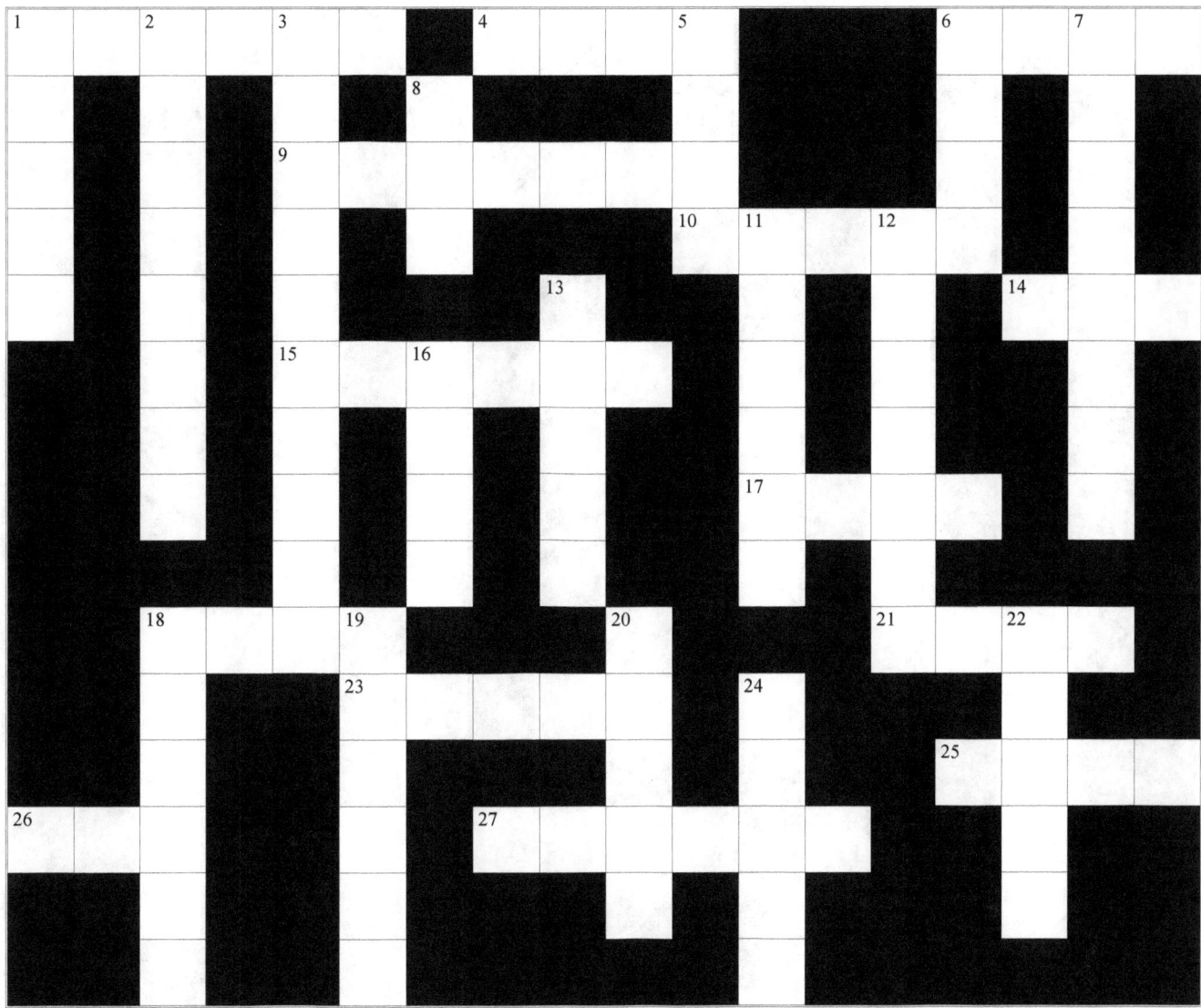

Across
1. Van Helsing instructs him to sit with Lucy through the night without leaving her.
4. The Count's is linked to Mina's.
6. Renfield's is broken.
9. Mrs. Westerna throws away Lucy's garlic ___.
10. Number of letters the Count instructs Jonathan to write home
14. Mina thinks she accidentally pricked Lucy with one.
15. Dracula owns ___, which is next door to Dr. Seward's place.
17. At midnight on St. George's Day all ___ things in the world have full sway.
18. She is engaged to marry Jonathan.
21. Communion wafer used as a weapon against vampires
23. Van Helsing compares Dracula to one.
25. She received 3 marriage proposals in one day.
26. Mina saw one flitting in the moonlight.
27. The Count escapes capture at Piccadilly by jumping our of this.

Down
1. One is driven through Lucy's heart.
2. Lucy's mother: Mrs. ___
3. The Count has no ___ in Jonathan's mirror.
5. The purified vampires turn to this.
6. These marks were found on the childrens' throats.
7. Hotel landlady gives Jonathan this for protection
8. A large one jumps off the ship and disappears in the dark.
11. He travels to Castle Dracula to meet with the Count about real estate.
12. The Count wants Jonathan to teach him this.
13. Home port of the Demeter
16. Dracula promises Renfield the lives of ____.
18. Renfield's name for the Count
19. Count Dracula claims to be a descendant of ___ the Hun.
20. Renfield stops himself before uttering this word.
22. Renfield wants life from other beings, not ___.
24. Renfield laps the Doctor's ___ off of the floor like a dog.

Dracula Crossword Answer Key

	1	2	3		4		5		6	7
1	S	E	W	A	R	D		M	I	N	D			B	A	C	K
2	T		E		E		8 D			U				I		R	
3	A		S	9 F	L	O	W	E	R	S				T		U	
4	K		T		L		G		10 T	11 H	12 R	E	E			C	
5	E		E		E		13 V		A		N			14 P	I	N
			R		15 C	16 A	R	F	A	X		G			F	
			N		T		A		R		17 E	L			I	
			A		I		T		N		V	I	L		X	
					O		S		A		R	S				
		18 M	I	19 N	A			20 D			21 H	O	22 S	T
		A		23 T	I	G	E	R		24 B			O	
		S		T				I		L		25 L	U	C	Y
26 B	A	T		I		27 W	I	N	D	O	W		L	
		E		L				K		O			S	
		R		A						D				

Across

1. Van Helsing instructs him to sit with Lucy through the night without leaving her.
4. The Count's is linked to Mina's.
6. Renfield's is broken.
9. Mrs. Westerna throws away Lucy's garlic ___.
10. Number of letters the Count instructs Jonathan to write home
14. Mina thinks she accidentally pricked Lucy with one.
15. Dracula owns ___, which is next door to Dr. Seward's place.
17. At midnight on St. George's Day all ___ things in the world have full sway.
18. She is engaged to marry Jonathan.
21. Communion wafer used as a weapon against vampires
23. Van Helsing compares Dracula to one.
25. She received 3 marriage proposals in one day.
26. Mina saw one flitting in the moonlight.
27. The Count escapes capture at Piccadilly by jumping out of this.

Down

1. One is driven through Lucy's heart.
2. Lucy's mother: Mrs. ____
3. The Count has no ___ in Jonathan's mirror.
5. The purified vampires turn to this.
6. These marks were found on the childrens' throats.
7. Hotel landlady gives Jonathan this for protection
8. A large one jumps off the ship and disappears in the dark.
11. He travels to Castle Dracula to meet with the Count about real estate.
12. The Count wants Jonathan to teach him this.
13. Home port of the Demeter
16. Dracula promises Renfield the lives of ____.
18. Renfield's name for the Count
19. Count Dracula claims to be a descendant of ___ the Hun.
20. Renfield stops himself before uttering this word.
22. Renfield wants life from other beings, not ___.
24. Renfield laps the Doctor's off of the floor like a dog.

Dracula Matching 1

___ 1. BURIAL A. Van Helsing compares Dracula to one.
___ 2. BAT B. Renfield wants life from other beings, not ___.
___ 3. CARFAX C. Lucy's mother: Mrs. ___
___ 4. DRINK D. She received 3 marriage proposals in one day.
___ 5. NOSFERATU E. Mina thinks she accidentally pricked Lucy with one.
___ 6. STRENGTH F. Renfield laps the Doctor's off of the floor like a dog.
___ 7. DUST G. Jonathan marvels at the caleche driver's
___ 8. TIGER H. Mina saw one flitting in the moonlight.
___ 9. QUINCY I. Renfield's is broken.
___10. BLOOD J. The Un-Dead
___11. MIRRORS K. Communion wafer used as a weapon against vampires
___12. GODALMING L. Arthur Holmwood: Lord ___
___13. SOULS M. There are none of these in the castle.
___14. VARNA N. He suggests that Lucy needs blood transfusions: Van ___
___15. TOMBSTONES O. American friend of Arthur Holmwood
___16. CHILD P. Jonathan hears the wail of a half-smothered ___ come from the bag.
___17. BACK Q. Renfield stops himself before uttering this word.
___18. WESTERNA R. Mina asks Jonathan to read the ___ Service for the Dead to her.
___19. HARKER S. Dracula owns ___, which is next door to Dr. Seward's place.
___20. NOTEBOOK T. Number of letters the Count instructs Jonathan to write home
___21. LUCY U. The old man claims these in the graveyard lie.
___22. PIN V. Home port of the Demeter
___23. THREE W. He travels to Castle Dracula to meet with the Count about real estate.
___24. HOST X. Mina promises not to tell Jonathan about the contents of his ___ unless it becomes necessary.
___25. HELSING Y. The purified vampires turn to this.

Dracula Matching 1 Answer Key

R - 1.	BURIAL	A. Van Helsing compares Dracula to one.
H - 2.	BAT	B. Renfield wants life from other beings, not ___.
S - 3.	CARFAX	C. Lucy's mother: Mrs. ___
Q - 4.	DRINK	D. She received 3 marriage proposals in one day.
J - 5.	NOSFERATU	E. Mina thinks she accidentally pricked Lucy with one.
G - 6.	STRENGTH	F. Renfield laps the Doctor's off of the floor like a dog.
Y - 7.	DUST	G. Jonathan marvels at the caleche driver's
A - 8.	TIGER	H. Mina saw one flitting in the moonlight.
O - 9.	QUINCY	I. Renfield's is broken.
F - 10.	BLOOD	J. The Un-Dead
M - 11.	MIRRORS	K. Communion wafer used as a weapon against vampires
L - 12.	GODALMING	L. Arthur Holmwood: Lord ___
B - 13.	SOULS	M. There are none of these in the castle.
V - 14.	VARNA	N. He suggests that Lucy needs blood transfusions: Van ___
U - 15.	TOMBSTONES	O. American friend of Arthur Holmwood
P - 16.	CHILD	P. Jonathan hears the wail of a half-smothered ___ come from the bag.
I - 17.	BACK	Q. Renfield stops himself before uttering this word.
C - 18.	WESTERNA	R. Mina asks Jonathan to read the ___ Service for the Dead to her.
W 19.	HARKER	S. Dracula owns ___, which is next door to Dr. Seward's place.
X - 20.	NOTEBOOK	T. Number of letters the Count instructs Jonathan to write home
D - 21.	LUCY	U. The old man claims these in the graveyard lie.
E - 22.	PIN	V. Home port of the Demeter
T - 23.	THREE	W. He travels to Castle Dracula to meet with the Count about real estate.
K - 24.	HOST	X. Mina promises not to tell Jonathan about the contents of his ___ unless it becomes necessary.
N - 25.	HELSING	Y. The purified vampires turn to this.

Dracula Matching 2

___ 1. HEAD   A. Count Dracula's home
___ 2. REFLECTION   B. One is driven through Lucy's heart.
___ 3. CAPTAIN   C. Communion wafer used as a weapon against vampires
___ 4. SEWARD   D. Jonathan hears the wail of a half-smothered ___ come from the bag.
___ 5. HOST   E. The Three voluptuous women are the ___ of Dracula.
___ 6. STAKE   F. Mina asks Jonathan to read the ___ Service for the Dead to her.
___ 7. HELSING   G. Mina promises not to tell Jonathan about the contents of his ___ unless it becomes necessary.
___ 8. WOLVES   H. Renfield wants life from other beings, not ___.
___ 9. FLOWERS   I. Children of the Night
___10. WINDOW   J. Van Helsing wants to cut off Lucy's ___ and take out her heart.
___11. SOULS   K. Renfield stops himself before uttering this word.
___12. DRINK   L. Renfield's is broken.
___13. BACK   M. The Count escapes capture at Piccadilly by jumping out of this.
___14. CHILD   N. These marks were found on the childrens' throats.
___15. BITE   O. The Count's is linked to Mina's.
___16. BRIDES   P. The body of the ___ was tied to the wheel of the ship.
___17. TIGER   Q. She received 3 marriage proposals in one day.
___18. MINA   R. The Count has no ___ in Jonathan's mirror.
___19. GODALMING   S. She is engaged to marry Jonathan.
___20. LUCY   T. The purified vampires turn to this.
___21. NOTEBOOK   U. Mrs. Westerna throws away Lucy's garlic ___.
___22. MIND   V. Van Helsing compares Dracula to one.
___23. TRANSYLVANIA W. Van Helsing instructs him to sit with Lucy through the night without leaving her.
___24. DUST   X. Arthur Holmwood: Lord ____
___25. BURIAL   Y. He suggests that Lucy needs blood transfusions: Van ___

Dracula Matching 2 Answer Key

J - 1.	HEAD	A. Count Dracula's home
R - 2.	REFLECTION	B. One is driven through Lucy's heart.
P - 3.	CAPTAIN	C. Communion wafer used as a weapon against vampires
W - 4.	SEWARD	D. Jonathan hears the wail of a half-smothered ___ come from the bag.
C - 5.	HOST	E. The Three voluptuous women are the ___ of Dracula.
B - 6.	STAKE	F. Mina asks Jonathan to read the ___ Service for the Dead to her.
Y - 7.	HELSING	G. Mina promises not to tell Jonathan about the contents of his ___ unless it becomes necessary.
I - 8.	WOLVES	H. Renfield wants life from other beings, not ___.
U - 9.	FLOWERS	I. Children of the Night
M - 10.	WINDOW	J. Van Helsing wants to cut off Lucy's ___ and take out her heart.
H - 11.	SOULS	K. Renfield stops himself before uttering this word.
K - 12.	DRINK	L. Renfield's is broken.
L - 13.	BACK	M. The Count escapes capture at Piccadilly by jumping out of this.
D - 14.	CHILD	N. These marks were found on the childrens' throats.
N - 15.	BITE	O. The Count's is linked to Mina's.
E - 16.	BRIDES	P. The body of the ___ was tied to the wheel of the ship.
V - 17.	TIGER	Q. She received 3 marriage proposals in one day.
S - 18.	MINA	R. The Count has no ___ in Jonathan's mirror.
X - 19.	GODALMING	S. She is engaged to marry Jonathan.
Q - 20.	LUCY	T. The purified vampires turn to this.
G - 21.	NOTEBOOK	U. Mrs. Westerna throws away Lucy's garlic ___.
O - 22.	MIND	V. Van Helsing compares Dracula to one.
A - 23.	TRANSYLVANIA	W. Van Helsing instructs him to sit with Lucy through the night without leaving her.
T - 24.	DUST	X. Arthur Holmwood: Lord ___
F - 25.	BURIAL	Y. He suggests that Lucy needs blood transfusions: Van ___

Dracula Juggle Letters

1. KETAS = 1. _____
One is driven through Lucy's heart.

2. RLBIAU = 2. _____
Mina asks Jonathan to read the ___ Service for the Dead to her.

3. ILGDOAMNG = 3. _____
Arthur Holmwood: Lord ____

4. EADH = 4. _____
Van Helsing wants to cut off Lucy's ___ and take out her heart.

5. ICLHD = 5. _____
Jonathan hears the wail of a half-smothered ___ come from the bag.

6. IMAN = 6. _____
She is engaged to marry Jonathan.

7. RCFXAA = 7. _____
Dracula owns ___, which is next door to Dr. Seward's place.

8. ESLIV = 8. _____
Renfield collects them.

9. SGHELNI = 9. _____
He suggests that Lucy needs blood transfusions: Van ___

10. DWRSAE =10. _____
Van Helsing instructs him to sit with Lucy through the night without leaving her.

11. NSLITVYARAAN =11. _____
Count Dracula's home

12. USTD =12. _____
The purified vampires turn to this.

13. LEIV =13. _____
At midnight on St. George's Day all ___ things in the world have full sway.

14. UXRCFCII =14. _____
Hotel landlady gives Jonathan this for protection

15. IGHLESN   =15. _____
                       The Count wants Jonathan to teach him this.

16. RHKRAE   =16. _____
                       He travels to Castle Dracula to meet with the Count about real estate.

17. VLWSOE   =17. _____
                       Children of the Night

18. NVAAR   =18. _____
                       Home port of the Demeter

19. OBNTOEOK   =19. _____
                       Mina promises not to tell Jonathan about the contents of his ___ unless it becomes necessary.

20. SOLSU   =20. _____
                       Renfield wants life from other beings, not ___.

21. RESISUN   =21. _____
                       Renfield is quiet from moonrise to ___.

22. TESTHNGR   =22. _____
                       Jonathan marvels at the caleche driver's

23. IBET   =23. _____
                       These marks were found on the childrens' throats.

24. IPN   =24. _____
                       Mina thinks she accidentally pricked Lucy with one.

25. IERTG   =25. _____
                       Van Helsing compares Dracula to one.

26. GDO   =26. _____
                       A large one jumps off the ship and disappears in the dark.

27. EERHT   =27. _____
                       Number of letters the Count instructs Jonathan to write home

28. ODLBO   =28. _____
                       Renfield laps the Doctor's off of the floor like a dog.

29. SEXBO   =29. _____
                       The Slovaks deliver large, wooden ___ with rope handles to the castle.

30. TBEONOTSMS =30. _____
   The old man claims these in the graveyard lie.

31. ATSR =31. _____
   Dracula promises Renfield the lives of ____.

32. IYUNCQ =32. _____
   American friend of Arthur Holmwood

33. OSEWRLF =33. _____
   Mrs. Westerna throws away Lucy's garlic ___.

34. OMHOWDLO =34. _____
   Lucy accepts his marriage proposal.

35. RMOSIRR =35. _____
   There are none of these in the castle.

36. HOST =36. _____
   Communion wafer used as a weapon against vampires

37. ILAATT =37. _____
   Count Dracula claims to be a descendant of ___ the Hun.

38. NAEERWTS =38. _____
   Lucy's mother: Mrs. ____

39. DINM =39. _____
   The Count's is linked to Mina's.

40. SNORUAFET =40. _____
   The Un-Dead

41. NIKRD =41. _____
   Renfield stops himself before uttering this word.

42. EDIBSR =42. _____
   The Three voluptuous women are the ___ of Dracula.

43. PACTNAI =43. _____
   The body of the ___ was tied to the wheel of the ship.

44. NWOWID =44. _____
   The Count escapes capture at Piccadilly by jumping out of this.

Dracula Juggle Letters Answer Key

1. KETAS = 1. STAKE
One is driven through Lucy's heart.

2. RLBIAU = 2. BURIAL
Mina asks Jonathan to read the ___ Service for the Dead to her.

3. ILGDOAMNG = 3. GODALMING
Arthur Holmwood: Lord ___

4. EADH = 4. HEAD
Van Helsing wants to cut off Lucy's ___ and take out her heart.

5. ICLHD = 5. CHILD
Jonathan hears the wail of a half-smothered ___ come from the bag.

6. IMAN = 6. MINA
She is engaged to marry Jonathan.

7. RCFXAA = 7. CARFAX
Dracula owns ___, which is next door to Dr. Seward's place.

8. ESLIV = 8. LIVES
Renfield collects them.

9. SGHELNI = 9. HELSING
He suggests that Lucy needs blood transfusions: Van ___

10. DWRSAE = 10. SEWARD
Van Helsing instructs him to sit with Lucy through the night without leaving her.

11. NSLITVYARAAN = 11. TRANSYLVANIA
Count Dracula's home

12. USTD = 12. DUST
The purified vampires turn to this.

13. LEIV = 13. EVIL
At midnight on St. George's Day all ___ things in the world have full sway.

14. UXRCFCII = 14. CRUCIFIX
Hotel landlady gives Jonathan this for protection

15. IGHLESN =15. ENGLISH
The Count wants Jonathan to teach him this.

16. RHKRAE =16. HARKER
He travels to Castle Dracula to meet with the Count about real estate.

17. VLWSOE =17. WOLVES
Children of the Night

18. NVAAR =18. VARNA
Home port of the Demeter

19. OBNTOEOK =19. NOTEBOOK
Mina promises not to tell Jonathan about the contents of his ___ unless it becomes necessary.

20. SOLSU =20. SOULS
Renfield wants life from other beings, not ___.

21. RESISUN =21. SUNRISE
Renfield is quiet from moonrise to ___.

22. TESTHNGR =22. STRENGTH
Jonathan marvels at the caleche driver's

23. IBET =23. BITE
These marks were found on the childrens' throats.

24. IPN =24. PIN
Mina thinks she accidentally pricked Lucy with one.

25. IERTG =25. TIGER
Van Helsing compares Dracula to one.

26. GDO =26. DOG
A large one jumps off the ship and disappears in the dark.

27. EERHT =27. THREE
Number of letters the Count instructs Jonathan to write home

28. ODLBO =28. BLOOD
Renfield laps the Doctor's off of the floor like a dog.

29. SEXBO =29. BOXES
The Slovaks deliver large, wooden ___ with rope handles to the castle.

30. TBEONOTSMS =30. TOMBSTONES

The old man claims these in the graveyard lie.

31. ATSR =31. RATS

Dracula promises Renfield the lives of ____.

32. IYUNCQ =32. QUINCY

American friend of Arthur Holmwood

33. OSEWRLF =33. FLOWERS

Mrs. Westerna throws away Lucy's garlic ____.

34. OMHOWDLO =34. HOLMWOOD

Lucy accepts his marriage proposal.

35. RMOSIRR =35. MIRRORS

There are none of these in the castle.

36. HOST =36. HOST

Communion wafer used as a weapon against vampires

37. ILAATT =37. ATTILA

Count Dracula claims to be a descendant of ____ the Hun.

38. NAEERWTS =38 WESTERNA

Lucy's mother: Mrs. ____

39. DINM =39. MIND

The Count's is linked to Mina's.

40. SNORUAFET =40. NOSFERATU

The Un-Dead

41. NIKRD =41. DRINK

Renfield stops himself before uttering this word.

42. EDIBSR =42. BRIDES

The Three voluptuous women are the ____ of Dracula.

43. PACTNAI =43. CAPTAIN

The body of the ____ was tied to the wheel of the ship.

44. NWOWID =44. WINDOW

The Count escapes capture at Piccadilly by jumping out of this.

VOCABULARY RESOURCE MATERIALS

Dracula Vocabulary Word List

No.	Word	Clue/Definition
1.	ABASEMENT	Low or downcast state
2.	ABATED	Reduced in amount, degree, or intensity
3.	ACCENTUATED	Stressed or emphasized; intensified
4.	ACQUIESCED	Consent or comply passively or without protest
5.	ACQUIESCED	Consented or complied passively or without protest
6.	ACUMEN	Quickness, accuracy, and keenness of judgment or insight
7.	ADDENDUM	Something added or to be added, as in a supplement to a book
8.	ADDUCE	Cite as an example or means of proof in an argument
9.	AFFLICT	Inflict grievous physical or mental suffering on
10.	AGGLOMERATION	Confused or jumbled mass
11.	AGUE	Chill or fit of shivering
12.	ALACRITY	Cheerful willingness; eagerness; speed or quickness
13.	AMENABLE	Responsive to advice, authority, or suggestion; willing
14.	ASCERTAIN	Make certain, definite, and precise
15.	ASSAIL	Attack, as with ridicule
16.	ASSIDUOUSLY	With care and persistence
17.	ASSIMILATION	Adopting the customs and attitudes of the prevailing culture
18.	AVARICE	Immoderate desire for wealth; greed
19.	BOUDOIR	Woman's private sitting room, dressing room, or bedroom
20.	CALECHE	Light carriage with two or four low wheels and a collapsible top
21.	CHAGRIN	Strong feelings of embarrassment
22.	CONSIGNING	Giving over to the care of another
23.	CONSTRAINED	In a forced or inhibited manner
24.	CONVERGED	Came together from different directions
25.	DEBAUCH	Corrupt morally
26.	DEFERENCE	Yielding to the opinion, wishes, or judgment of another
27.	DEMURRED	Voiced opposition; objected
28.	DESPATCH	Written, official message sent with speed
29.	DIORAMA	Scene in which figures are arranged in a naturalistic setting against a painted background
30.	DISPOSITION	One's usual mood; temperament
31.	DISSIPATED	Drove away; dispersed
32.	DISTILS	Separates or purifies
33.	ELUDE	Evade or escape from, as by daring, cleverness, or skill
34.	EMACIATED	Extremely thin, especially as a result of starvation
35.	EMINENCE	Position of great distinction or superiority
36.	ENIGMATICAL	Puzzling or mysterious
37.	ENTAILED	Limited inheritance of property to specified heirs
38.	EXPOSTULATE	Reason with someone in an effort to dissuade or correct
39.	FISSURE	Long, narrow opening; a crack or cleft
40.	HAGGARD	Appearing worn and exhausted
41.	HOODWINK	Take in by deceptive means; deceive
42.	HUSBANDRY	Practice of growing crops, & breeding and raising livestock
43.	IMPERTURBABLE	Unshakably calm and collected
44.	IMPLICITLY	In a manner which is understood though not directly expressed
45.	IMPOTENT	Lacking physical strength or vigor; weak
46.	IMPREGNABLE	Impossible to capture or enter by force
47.	INQUIETUDE	State of restlessness or uneasiness
48.	INQUISITION	The act of inquiring into a matter; an investigation
49.	INSTIGATION	Deliberate triggering of trouble or discord

50.	INTRIGUED	Engaged in secret or underhanded schemes
51.	IRKSOME	Causing annoyance, weariness, or vexation
52.	LAIR	Den or dwelling of a wild animal; a hideaway
53.	LANGUID	Lacking energy or vitality; weak
54.	MAELSTROM	Violent or turbulent situation; a large, violent whirlpool
55.	MALADY	Disease, disorder, or ailment
56.	MALIGNITY	Intense ill will or hatred; great malice
57.	MALODOROUS	Having a bad odor; foul
58.	MENIAL	Relating to work regarded as for a servant
59.	MUNDANE	Relating to commonplace things; ordinary
60.	ODIUM	Strong dislike, contempt or aversion
61.	PALLOR	Extreme or unnatural paleness
62.	PAROXYSM	Sudden outburst of emotion or action
63.	PLACIDITY	Quality of being undisturbed by tumult or disorder; relaxation
64.	POIGNANT	Distressing to the mind or feelings; profoundly moving or touching
65.	PORTERAGE	Charge for the carrying of burdens or goods as done by porters
66.	PRESAGE	Indication or warning of a future occurrence; an omen
67.	PRODIGIOUS	Impressively great in size, force, or extent; enormous
68.	PROLIFIC	Producing abundant works or results
69.	PROSAIC	Matter-of-fact; straightforward; lacking imagination; dull
70.	QUERIED	Questioned; inquired
71.	REMONSTRANCE	Expression of protest or complaint
72.	REPUDIATED	Rejected emphatically as unfounded, untrue, or unjust
73.	REQUISITIONS	Formal, written requests for something needed
74.	RESONANT	Strong and deep in tone
75.	RESUMPTION	Beginning again
76.	RETICENT	Inclined to keep one's thoughts, feelings, and personal affairs to oneself
77.	REVERENTLY	In a state of profound awe and respect and often love
78.	SANGUINE	Cheerfully confident; optimistic; of a healthy reddish color
79.	SATURNINE	Melancholy or sullen; tending to be bitter
80.	SEXTON	Employee responsible for the upkeep of church property
81.	SMOTE	Struck down or hit
82.	SOPHISTIC	Characteristic of a scholar or thinker
83.	STALWART	Having or marked by imposing physical strength
84.	SUCCUMBED	Yielded to an overwhelming desire; gave up or gave in
85.	TACIT	Not spoken
86.	TETHER	Restrain for holding an animal in place
87.	THWARTING	Opposing and defeating the efforts, plans, or ambitions of something
88.	TORRENT	Heavy, uncontrolled outpouring
89.	TRENCHANT	Forceful, effective, and vigorous
90.	TUMULT	Agitation of the mind or emotions
91.	UNFETTERED	Set free or kept free from restrictions or bonds
92.	UNHALLOWED	Unholy
93.	URBANE	Polite, refined, and often elegant in manner
94.	VERBATIM	In exactly the same words; word for word
95.	VIADUCT	Bridge consisting of arches used to carry a road over a valley
96.	VOLUPTUOUS	Arising from or contributing to the satisfaction of sensual desires
97.	WILY	Marked by skill in deception

Dracula Vocabulary Word Search

```
U D E T A B A G G L O M E R A T I O N F S
N I G C H K K L M Y A G A S V S A V B H R
H S A I R W D C A D S N C L Z I S C G N F
A S S L S P A Q M C U E G X I T A A I V G
L I E F F A C R I G R H D U L G E D I T N
L P R F Z L U M T T B I V E I N N K U L O
O A P A N L M K A I A P T Q M D I I P C I
W T S Y O O E I B R N D A Y H U N T T X T
E E L A I R N T R V E G D M Q P R O Z Y I
D D B Y T S L I E K J E D U C K U R H K S
E U C P P U O Y V H F N E T C T T R E H O
B L L R M D E A N E G R N T E E A E W D P
M E P U U J M M R R I V D N F T S N I L S
U D T O S D I E W E E G U A D Q H T L K I
C R B H E H N N D L D Q M N G N X E Y P D
C B E H R C E A C R L J U G O D B F R Y V
U H H T E Y N B M D E P Y I V E W O Y K H
S X A H I D C L A E R S T O S L L H D U C
A Y G G V C E E E U L A O P P I D J S B U
N Y G F R K E M L G G Z J N F A T B J Q A
G M A P M I Q N S I H X H I A T A I N P B
U J R E M O N S T R A N C E R N S M O T E
I Y D A L A M S R T R G B P D E T V H N D
N M U N D A N E O N M W U R M E N I A L S
E D I S T I L S M I R K Y E O D I U M X C
```

ABATED	DEMURRED	MALIGNITY	SATURNINE
ACUMEN	DISPOSITION	MENIAL	SMOTE
ADDENDUM	DISSIPATED	MUNDANE	SUCCUMBED
ADDUCE	DISTILS	ODIUM	TACIT
AFFLICT	ELUDE	PALLOR	TETHER
AGGLOMERATION	EMINENCE	POIGNANT	THWARTING
AGUE	ENTAILED	PRESAGE	TORRENT
ALACRITY	HAGGARD	PROLIFIC	TUMULT
AMENABLE	HUSBANDRY	QUERIED	UNHALLOWED
ASCERTAIN	INSTIGATION	REMONSTRANCE	URBANE
ASSAIL	INTRIGUED	REQUISITIONS	VERBATIM
BOUDOIR	LAIR	RESONANT	VIADUCT
CHAGRIN	LANGUID	RESUMPTION	WILY
DEBAUCH	MAELSTROM	RETICENT	
DEFERENCE	MALADY	SANGUINE	

Dracula Vocabulary Word Search Answer Key

ABATED	DEMURRED	MALIGNITY	SATURNINE
ACUMEN	DISPOSITION	MENIAL	SMOTE
ADDENDUM	DISSIPATED	MUNDANE	SUCCUMBED
ADDUCE	DISTILS	ODIUM	TACIT
AFFLICT	ELUDE	PALLOR	TETHER
AGGLOMERATION	EMINENCE	POIGNANT	THWARTING
AGUE	ENTAILED	PRESAGE	TORRENT
ALACRITY	HAGGARD	PROLIFIC	TUMULT
AMENABLE	HUSBANDRY	QUERIED	UNHALLOWED
ASCERTAIN	INSTIGATION	REMONSTRANCE	URBANE
ASSAIL	INTRIGUED	REQUISITIONS	VERBATIM
BOUDOIR	LAIR	RESONANT	VIADUCT
CHAGRIN	LANGUID	RESUMPTION	WILY
DEBAUCH	MAELSTROM	RETICENT	
DEFERENCE	MALADY	SANGUINE	

Dracula Vocabulary Crossword

Across
- 4. Restrain for holding an animal in place
- 6. Impressively great in size, force, or extent; enormous
- 11. Lacking physical strength or vigor; weak
- 12. Agitation of the mind or emotions
- 13. Disease, disorder, or ailment
- 15. Came together from different directions
- 16. Marked by skill in deception
- 17. Den or dwelling of a wild animal; a hideaway
- 18. Sudden outburst of emotion or action
- 19. Bridge consisting of arches used to carry a road over a valley
- 23. Quickness, accuracy, and keenness of judgment or insight
- 24. Unshakably calm and collected
- 25. Employee responsible for the upkeep of church property
- 26. Relating to commonplace things; ordinary

Down
- 1. Strong and deep in tone
- 2. Chill or fit of shivering
- 3. In a forced or inhibited manner
- 5. Puzzling or mysterious
- 7. Inclined to keep one's thoughts, feelings, and personal affairs to oneself
- 8. Voiced opposition; objected
- 9. Strong dislike, contempt or aversion
- 10. Melancholy or sullen; tending to be bitter
- 14. Appearing worn and exhausted
- 15. Giving over to the care of another
- 20. Reduced in amount, degree, or intensity
- 21. Extreme or unnatural paleness
- 22. Struck down or hit

Dracula Vocabulary Crossword Answer Key

Across
- 4. Restrain for holding an animal in place
- 6. Impressively great in size, force, or extent; enormous
- 11. Lacking physical strength or vigor; weak
- 12. Agitation of the mind or emotions
- 13. Disease, disorder, or ailment
- 15. Came together from different directions
- 16. Marked by skill in deception
- 17. Den or dwelling of a wild animal; a hideaway
- 18. Sudden outburst of emotion or action
- 19. Bridge consisting of arches used to carry a road over a valley
- 23. Quickness, accuracy, and keenness of judgment or insight
- 24. Unshakably calm and collected
- 25. Employee responsible for the upkeep of church property
- 26. Relating to commonplace things; ordinary

Down
- 1. Strong and deep in tone
- 2. Chill or fit of shivering
- 3. In a forced or inhibited manner
- 5. Puzzling or mysterious
- 7. Inclined to keep one's thoughts, feelings, and personal affairs to oneself
- 8. Voiced opposition; objected
- 9. Strong dislike, contempt or aversion
- 10. Melancholy or sullen; tending to be bitter
- 14. Appearing worn and exhausted
- 15. Giving over to the care of another
- 20. Reduced in amount, degree, or intensity
- 21. Extreme or unnatural paleness
- 22. Struck down or hit

Answers

Across: 4. TETHER, 6. PRODIGIOUS, 11. IMPOTENT, 12. TUMULT, 13. MALADY, 15. CONVERGED, 16. WILY, 17. LAIR, 18. PAROXYSM, 19. VIADUCT, 23. ACUMEN, 24. IMPERTURBABLE, 25. SEXTON, 26. MUNDANE

Down: 1. RESONANT, 2. AGUE, 3. CONSTRAINEDLY, 5. ENIGMATIC, 7. RETICENT, 8. DEMURRED, 9. REPUGNANCE, 10. SATURNINE, 14. HAGGARD, 15. CONSIGNED, 20. ABATED, 21. PALLOR, 22. SMOTE

Dracula Vocabulary Matching 1

___ 1. REPUDIATED   A. Unshakably calm and collected
___ 2. FISSURE   B. Causing annoyance, weariness, or vexation
___ 3. PALLOR   C. Extremely thin, especially as a result of starvation
___ 4. LAIR   D. Long, narrow opening; a crack or cleft
___ 5. IMPERTURBABLE   E. Rejected emphatically as unfounded, untrue, or unjust
___ 6. AGGLOMERATION   F. Deliberate triggering of trouble or discord
___ 7. RESONANT   G. Charge for the carrying of burdens or goods as done by porters
___ 8. PORTERAGE   H. Den or dwelling of a wild animal; a hideaway
___ 9. POIGNANT   I. Reduced in amount, degree, or intensity
___ 10. ODIUM   J. Extreme or unnatural paleness
___ 11. TETHER   K. Giving over to the care of another
___ 12. IRKSOME   L. Restrain for holding an animal in place
___ 13. EMACIATED   M. Cite as an example or means of proof in an argument
___ 14. ACQUIESCED   N. Make certain, definite, and precise
___ 15. TORRENT   O. Heavy, uncontrolled outpouring
___ 16. VIADUCT   P. Bridge consisting of arches used to carry a road over a valley
___ 17. ASCERTAIN   Q. Strong dislike, contempt or aversion
___ 18. UNFETTERED   R. Questioned; inquired
___ 19. TRENCHANT   S. Strong and deep in tone
___ 20. INSTIGATION   T. Consented or complied passively or without protest
___ 21. ABATED   U. Distressing to the mind or feelings; profoundly moving or touching
___ 22. QUERIED   V. Forceful, effective, and vigorous
___ 23. ADDUCE   W. Set free or kept free from restrictions or bonds
___ 24. THWARTING   X. Opposing and defeating the efforts, plans, or ambitions of something
___ 25. CONSIGNING   Y. Confused or jumbled mass

Dracula Vocabulary Matching 1 Answer Key

E - 1.	REPUDIATED	A. Unshakably calm and collected
D - 2.	FISSURE	B. Causing annoyance, weariness, or vexation
J - 3.	PALLOR	C. Extremely thin, especially as a result of starvation
H - 4.	LAIR	D. Long, narrow opening; a crack or cleft
A - 5.	IMPERTURBABLE	E. Rejected emphatically as unfounded, untrue, or unjust
Y - 6.	AGGLOMERATION	F. Deliberate triggering of trouble or discord
S - 7.	RESONANT	G. Charge for the carrying of burdens or goods as done by porters
G - 8.	PORTERAGE	H. Den or dwelling of a wild animal; a hideaway
U - 9.	POIGNANT	I. Reduced in amount, degree, or intensity
Q -10.	ODIUM	J. Extreme or unnatural paleness
L -11.	TETHER	K. Giving over to the care of another
B -12.	IRKSOME	L. Restrain for holding an animal in place
C -13.	EMACIATED	M. Cite as an example or means of proof in an argument
T -14.	ACQUIESCED	N. Make certain, definite, and precise
O -15.	TORRENT	O. Heavy, uncontrolled outpouring
P -16.	VIADUCT	P. Bridge consisting of arches used to carry a road over a valley
N -17.	ASCERTAIN	Q. Strong dislike, contempt or aversion
W -18.	UNFETTERED	R. Questioned; inquired
V -19.	TRENCHANT	S. Strong and deep in tone
F -20.	INSTIGATION	T. Consented or complied passively or without protest
I -21.	ABATED	U. Distressing to the mind or feelings; profoundly moving or touching
R -22.	QUERIED	V. Forceful, effective, and vigorous
M -23.	ADDUCE	W. Set free or kept free from restrictions or bonds
X -24.	THWARTING	X. Opposing and defeating the efforts, plans, or ambitions of something
K -25.	CONSIGNING	Y. Confused or jumbled mass

Dracula Vocabulary Matching 2

___ 1. DEFERENCE   A. In a manner which is understood though not directly expressed

___ 2. BOUDOIR   B. Position of great distinction or superiority

___ 3. UNHALLOWED   C. Having a bad odor; foul

___ 4. RETICENT   D. In exactly the same words; word for word

___ 5. IMPLICITLY   E. Causing annoyance, weariness, or vexation

___ 6. ENTAILED   F. Relating to commonplace things; ordinary

___ 7. DEBAUCH   G. Agitation of the mind or emotions

___ 8. PROSAIC   H. Impossible to capture or enter by force

___ 9. PALLOR   I. Unholy

___ 10. TUMULT   J. Disease, disorder, or ailment

___ 11. DEMURRED   K. Reason with someone in an effort to dissuade or correct

___ 12. EXPOSTULATE   L. Corrupt morally

___ 13. STALWART   M. Adopting the customs and attitudes of the prevailing culture

___ 14. MUNDANE   N. Characteristic of a scholar or thinker

___ 15. SOPHISTIC   O. Extreme or unnatural paleness

___ 16. VERBATIM   P. Limited inheritance of property to specified heirs

___ 17. IMPREGNABLE   Q. Yielding to the opinion, wishes, or judgment of another

___ 18. ASSIMILATION   R. Inclined to keep one's thoughts, feelings, and personal affairs to oneself

___ 19. MALADY   S. Matter-of-fact; straightforward; lacking imagination; dull

___ 20. LAIR   T. Woman's private sitting room, dressing room, or bedroom

___ 21. HUSBANDRY   U. Practice of growing crops, & breeding and raising livestock

___ 22. DESPATCH   V. Voiced opposition; objected

___ 23. EMINENCE   W. Written, official message sent with speed

___ 24. MALODOROUS   X. Having or marked by imposing physical strength

___ 25. IRKSOME   Y. Den or dwelling of a wild animal; a hideaway

Dracula Vocabulary Matching 2 Answer Key

Q - 1.	DEFERENCE	A. In a manner which is understood though not directly expressed
T - 2.	BOUDOIR	B. Position of great distinction or superiority
I - 3.	UNHALLOWED	C. Having a bad odor; foul
R - 4.	RETICENT	D. In exactly the same words; word for word
A - 5.	IMPLICITLY	E. Causing annoyance, weariness, or vexation
P - 6.	ENTAILED	F. Relating to commonplace things; ordinary
L - 7.	DEBAUCH	G. Agitation of the mind or emotions
S - 8.	PROSAIC	H. Impossible to capture or enter by force
O - 9.	PALLOR	I. Unholy
G - 10.	TUMULT	J. Disease, disorder, or ailment
V - 11.	DEMURRED	K. Reason with someone in an effort to dissuade or correct
K - 12.	EXPOSTULATE	L. Corrupt morally
X - 13.	STALWART	M. Adopting the customs and attitudes of the prevailing culture
F - 14.	MUNDANE	N. Characteristic of a scholar or thinker
N - 15.	SOPHISTIC	O. Extreme or unnatural paleness
D - 16.	VERBATIM	P. Limited inheritance of property to specified heirs
H - 17.	IMPREGNABLE	Q. Yielding to the opinion, wishes, or judgment of another
M - 18.	ASSIMILATION	R. Inclined to keep one's thoughts, feelings, and personal affairs to oneself
J - 19.	MALADY	S. Matter-of-fact; straightforward; lacking imagination; dull
Y - 20.	LAIR	T. Woman's private sitting room, dressing room, or bedroom
U - 21.	HUSBANDRY	U. Practice of growing crops, & breeding and raising livestock
W - 22.	DESPATCH	V. Voiced opposition; objected
B - 23.	EMINENCE	W. Written, official message sent with speed
C - 24.	MALODOROUS	X. Having or marked by imposing physical strength
E - 25.	IRKSOME	Y. Den or dwelling of a wild animal; a hideaway

Dracula Vocabulary Juggle Letters

1. ULINGAD = 1. _____
Lacking energy or vitality; weak

2. ROGNVEDEC = 2. _____
Came together from different directions

3. NTIONDCSARE = 3. _____
In a forced or inhibited manner

4. MATVERBI = 4. _____
In exactly the same words; word for word

5. LADROUMOSO = 5. _____
Having a bad odor; foul

6. MBCUSDCEU = 6. _____
Yielded to an overwhelming desire; gave up or gave in

7. GGHDARA = 7. _____
Appearing worn and exhausted

8. UNYHBRDAS = 8. _____
Practice of growing crops, & breeding and raising livestock

9. ESGPREA = 9. _____
Indication or warning of a future occurrence; an omen

10. MAECNU =10. _____
Quickness, accuracy, and keenness of judgment or insight

11. UDTCAIV =11. _____
Bridge consisting of arches used to carry a road over a valley

12. ATSEPOELTXU =12. _____
Reason with someone in an effort to dissuade or correct

13. ACITFLF =13. _____
Inflict grievous physical or mental suffering on

14. SGPRDIUIOO =14. _____
Impressively great in size, force, or extent; enormous

15. TBAREUIPELRBM =15. _____
Unshakably calm and collected

16. CSDETHPA =16. _____
Written, official message sent with speed

17. ENNEMECI =17. _____
Position of great distinction or superiority

18. BEEPNMIRLGA =18. _____
Impossible to capture or enter by force

19. TGTSIONIANI =19. _____
Deliberate triggering of trouble or discord

20. TSIEQIONRIUS =20. _____
Formal, written requests for something needed

21. EDMETICAA =21. _____
Extremely thin, especially as a result of starvation

22. LNEEBAAM =22. _____
Responsive to advice, authority, or suggestion; willing

23. INGCHAR =23. _____
Strong feelings of embarrassment

24. RNHNETCAT =24. _____
Forceful, effective, and vigorous

25. NAERTOSN =25. _____
Strong and deep in tone

26. ERMSOIK =26. _____
Causing annoyance, weariness, or vexation

27. EARNUB =27. _____
Polite, refined, and often elegant in manner

28. OHSPICTSI =28. _____
Characteristic of a scholar or thinker

29. TXNEOS =29. _____
Employee responsible for the upkeep of church property

30. ITISDSL =30. _____
Separates or purifies

31. RWIANTTHG =31. _____
Opposing and defeating the efforts, plans, or ambitions of something

32. ATCIT =32. _____
Not spoken

33. EDELU =33. _____
Evade or escape from, as by daring, cleverness, or skill

34. UUTLTM =34. _____
Agitation of the mind or emotions

35. FREISSU =35. _____
Long, narrow opening; a crack or cleft

36. CIRETNET =36. _____
Inclined to keep one's thoughts, feelings, and personal affairs to oneself

37. WYLI =37. _____
Marked by skill in deception

38. MAOYPRXS =38. _____
Sudden outburst of emotion or action

39. LATMNIGYI =39. _____
Intense ill will or hatred; great malice

40. TALGEGOINMORA =40. _____
Confused or jumbled mass

41. ABDTEA =41. _____
Reduced in amount, degree, or intensity

42. NINCONGSGI =42. _____
Giving over to the care of another

43. NIRSCAATE =43. _____
Make certain, definite, and precise

44. OUDROIB =44. _____
Woman's private sitting room, dressing room, or bedroom

45. RNTROTE =45. _____
Heavy, uncontrolled outpouring

46. WNDKHIOO =46. _____
Take in by deceptive means; deceive

Dracula Vocabulary Juggle Letters Answer Key

1. ULINGAD = 1. LANGUID
   Lacking energy or vitality; weak

2. ROGNVEDEC = 2. CONVERGED
   Came together from different directions

3. NTIONDCSARE = 3. CONSTRAINED
   In a forced or inhibited manner

4. MATVERBI = 4. VERBATIM
   In exactly the same words; word for word

5. LADROUMOSO = 5. MALODOROUS
   Having a bad odor; foul

6. MBCUSDCEU = 6. SUCCUMBED
   Yielded to an overwhelming desire; gave up or gave in

7. GGHDARA = 7. HAGGARD
   Appearing worn and exhausted

8. UNYHBRDAS = 8. HUSBANDRY
   Practice of growing crops, & breeding and raising livestock

9. ESGPREA = 9. PRESAGE
   Indication or warning of a future occurrence; an omen

10. MAECNU = 10. ACUMEN
    Quickness, accuracy, and keenness of judgment or insight

11. UDTCAIV = 11. VIADUCT
    Bridge consisting of arches used to carry a road over a valley

12. ATSEPOELTXU = 12. EXPOSTULATE
    Reason with someone in an effort to dissuade or correct

13. ACITFLF = 13. AFFLICT
    Inflict grievous physical or mental suffering on

14. SGPRDIUIOO = 14. PRODIGIOUS
    Impressively great in size, force, or extent; enormous

15. TBAREUIPELRBM = 15. IMPERTURBABLE
    Unshakably calm and collected

16. CSDETHPA =16. DESPATCH
Written, official message sent with speed

17. ENNEMECI =17. EMINENCE
Position of great distinction or superiority

18. BEEPNMIRLGA =18. IMPREGNABLE
Impossible to capture or enter by force

19. TGTSIONIANI =19. INSTIGATION
Deliberate triggering of trouble or discord

20. TSIEQIONRIUS =20. REQUISITIONS
Formal, written requests for something needed

21. EDMETICAA =21. EMACIATED
Extremely thin, especially as a result of starvation

22. LNEEBAAM =22. AMENABLE
Responsive to advice, authority, or suggestion; willing

23. INGCHAR =23. CHAGRIN
Strong feelings of embarrassment

24. RNHNETCAT =24. TRENCHANT
Forceful, effective, and vigorous

25. NAERTOSN =25. RESONANT
Strong and deep in tone

26. ERMSOIK =26. IRKSOME
Causing annoyance, weariness, or vexation

27. EARNUB =27. URBANE
Polite, refined, and often elegant in manner

28. OHSPICTSI =28. SOPHISTIC
Characteristic of a scholar or thinker

29. TXNEOS =29. SEXTON
Employee responsible for the upkeep of church property

30. ITISDSL =30. DISTILS
Separates or purifies

31. RWIANTTHG =31. THWARTING
Opposing and defeating the efforts, plans, or ambitions of something

32. ATCIT =32. TACIT
Not spoken

33. EDELU =33. ELUDE
Evade or escape from, as by daring, cleverness, or skill

34. UUTLTM =34. TUMULT
Agitation of the mind or emotions

35. FREISSU =35. FISSURE
Long, narrow opening; a crack or cleft

36. CIRETNET =36. RETICENT
Inclined to keep one's thoughts, feelings, and personal affairs to oneself

37. WYLI =37. WILY
Marked by skill in deception

38. MAOYPRXS =38. PAROXYSM
Sudden outburst of emotion or action

39. LATMNIGYI =39. MALIGNITY
Intense ill will or hatred; great malice

40. TALGEGOINMORA =40. AGGLOMERATION
Confused or jumbled mass

41. ABDTEA =41. ABATED
Reduced in amount, degree, or intensity

42. NINCONGSGI =42. CONSIGNING
Giving over to the care of another

43. NIRSCAATE =43. ASCERTAIN
Make certain, definite, and precise

44. OUDROIB =44. BOUDOIR
Woman's private sitting room, dressing room, or bedroom

45. RNTROTE =45. TORRENT
Heavy, uncontrolled outpouring

46. WNDKHIOO =46. HOODWINK
Take in by deceptive means; deceive